For a Left Populism

For a Left Populism

Chantal Mouffe

VERSO
London • New York

First published by Verso 2018
© Chantal Mouffe 2018

1 3 5 7 9 10 8 6 4 2

Verso
UK: 6 Meard Street, London W1F 0EG
US: 20 Jay Street, Suite 1010, Brooklyn, NY 11201
versobooks.com

Verso is the imprint of New Left Books

ISBN-13: 978-1-78663-755-0
ISBN-13: 978-1-78663-757-4 (UK EBK)
ISBN-13: 978-1-78663-758-1 (US EBK)

British Library Cataloguing in Publication Data
A catalogue record for this book is available from the British Library

Library of Congress Cataloging-in-Publication Data
A catalog record for this book is available from the Library of Congress

Typeset in Sabon by Hewer Text UK Ltd, Edinburgh
Printed in and bound by CPI Group (UK) Ltd, Croydon, CR0 4YY

to Ernesto

Men can second fortune, but not oppose it . . . They can weave its warp but not break it. They should indeed never give up for, since they do not know its end and it proceeds by oblique and unknown ways, they have always to hope and, since they hope, not to give up in whatever fortune and in whatever travail they may find themselves.

– Niccolò Machiavelli, *Discourses on Livy*

Contents

Introduction   1
1 The Populist Moment   9
2 Learning from Thatcherism   25
3 Radicalizing Democracy   39
4 The Construction of a People   59
Conclusion   79
Theoretical Appendix   87
Acknowledgements   95
Index   97

Introduction

At the origin of this book is my conviction that it is urgent for the left to grasp the nature of the current conjuncture and the challenge represented by the 'populist moment'. We are witnessing a crisis of the neoliberal hegemonic formation and this crisis opens the possibility for the construction of a more democratic order. To be able to seize this opportunity, it is essential to come to terms with the nature of the transformations undergone in the last thirty years and their consequences for democratic politics.

I am convinced that so many socialist and social-democratic parties are in disarray because they stick to an inadequate conception of politics, a conception whose critique has been at the centre of my reflection for many years. This critique was initiated in *Hegemony and Socialist Strategy: Towards a Radical Democratic Politics*, written jointly with Ernesto Laclau and published in 1985.

What motivated us was the incapacity of left politics, both in its Marxist and social-democratic versions, to take account of a series of movements that had emerged in the wake of the 1968 revolts and that corresponded to resistances against a variety of forms of domination which could not be formulated in class terms. The second wave of feminism, the gay movement, the anti-racist struggles and issues around the environment had profoundly transformed the political panorama, but the traditional left parties were not receptive to those demands whose political character they were unable to acknowledge. It was in view of remedying those shortcomings that we decided to enquire about the reasons for such a situation.

We soon realized that the obstacles to be overcome came from the essentialist perspective dominant in left thinking. According to this perspective, that we called 'class essentialism', political identities were the expression of the position of the social agents in the relations of production and their interests were defined by this position. It was no surprise that such a perspective was unable to understand demands that were not based on 'class'.

An important part of the book was dedicated to refuting this essentialist approach, utilizing insights from poststructuralism. Combining those insights with those of Antonio Gramsci, we developed an alternative 'anti-essentialist' approach apt to grasp the multiplicity of struggles against different forms of domination. To give a political expression to the articulation of those struggles, we proposed redefining the socialist project in terms of a 'radicalization of democracy'.

Such a project consisted in the establishment of a 'chain of equivalences' articulating the demands of the working class with those of the new movements in order to construct a 'common will' aiming at the creation of what Gramsci called an 'expansive hegemony'. By reformulating the project of the left in terms of 'radical and plural democracy', we inscribed it in the wider field of the democratic revolution, indicating that multiple struggles for emancipation are founded on the plurality of social agents and of their struggles. The field of social conflict was thereby extended rather than being concentrated in a 'privileged agent' like the working class. To be clear, contrary to some disingenuous readings of our argument, this does not mean we privilege the demands of the new movements at the expense of those of the working class. What we stressed was the need for a left politics to articulate the struggles about different forms of subordination without attributing any *a priori* centrality to any of them.

We also indicated that the extension and radicalization of democratic struggles would never achieve a fully liberated society and the emancipatory project could not be conceived any longer as the elimination of the state. There will always be antagonisms, struggles and partial opaqueness of the social. This is why the myth of communism as a transparent and reconciled society – clearly implying the end of politics – had to be abandoned.

The book was written in a conjuncture marked by the crisis of the social-democratic hegemonic formation established during the postwar years. Social-democratic values were being challenged by the neoliberal offensive, but they were still influential in shaping Western European common sense and our objective was to envisage how to defend and radicalize them. Alas, when the second edition of *Hegemony and Socialist Strategy* came out in 2000, we noted in the new introduction that in the fifteen years since its original publication, a serious regression had taken place. Under the pretence of 'modernization', an increasing number of social-democratic parties had discarded their 'left' identity and had euphemistically redefined themselves as 'centre-left'.

It was this new conjuncture that I analyzed in *On the Political*, published in 2005, where I examined the impact of the 'third way' theorized in Britain by Anthony Giddens and implemented by Tony Blair and his New Labour Party. I showed how, having accepted the hegemonic terrain established by Margaret Thatcher around the dogma that there was no alternative to neoliberal globalization, her famous 'TINA', the new centre-left government ended up implementing what Stuart Hall has called a 'social-democratic version of neoliberalism'. By claiming that the adversarial model of politics and the left/right opposition had become obsolete, and by celebrating the 'consensus at the centre' between centre-right and centre-left, the so-called 'radical centre' promoted a technocratic form of politics according to which politics was not a partisan confrontation but the neutral management of public affairs.

As Tony Blair used to say: 'The choice is not between a left-wing economic policy and a right-wing one but between a good economic policy and a bad one.' Neoliberal globalization was seen as a fate that we had to accept, and political questions were reduced to mere technical issues to be dealt with by experts. No space was left for the citizens to have a real choice between different political projects and their role was limited to approving the 'rational' policies elaborated by those experts.

Contrary to those who presented such a situation as progress for a maturing democracy, I argued that this 'post-political' situation was the origin of a process of disaffection with democratic institutions, manifested in the increasing level of abstention. I also warned against the growing success of right-wing populist parties pretending to offer an alternative that gave back to the people the voice that had been confiscated by the establishment elites. I insisted on the need to break with the post-political consensus and to reaffirm the partisan nature of politics in order to create the conditions of an 'agonistic' debate about possible alternatives.

At that time, as I now realize, I was still thinking that socialist and social-democratic parties could be transformed in order to implement the project of radicalization of democracy that we were advocating in *Hegemony and Socialist Strategy*.

Clearly this did not happen and social-democratic parties have entered into a process of decline in most Western European democracies, while important inroads have been made by right-wing populism. However, the 2008 economic crisis brought to the fore the contradictions of the neoliberal model and today the neoliberal hegemonic formation is being called into question by a variety of anti-establishment movements, both from the right and from the left. This is the new conjuncture, which I will call the 'populist moment', that I intend to scrutinize here.

The central argument of this book is that to intervene in the hegemonic crisis, it is necessary to establish a political frontier and that left populism, understood as a discursive strategy of construction of the political frontier between 'the people' and 'the oligarchy', constitutes, in the present conjuncture, the type of politics needed to recover and deepen democracy.

When I wrote *On the Political* I suggested reviving the left/right frontier, but I am now convinced that, as traditionally configured, such a frontier is no longer adequate to articulate a collective will that contains the variety of democratic demands that exist today. The populist moment is the expression of a set of heterogeneous demands, which cannot be formulated merely in terms of interests linked to determinate social categories. Furthermore, in neoliberal capitalism new forms of subordination have emerged outside the productive process. They have given rise to demands that no longer correspond to social sectors defined in sociological terms and by their location in the social structure. Such claims – the defence of the environment, struggles against sexism, racism and other forms of domination – have become increasingly central. This is why today the political frontier needs to be constructed in a 'populist' transversal mode. Nevertheless, I will also argue that the 'populist' dimension is not sufficient to specify the type of politics required by the current conjuncture. It needs to be qualified as a 'left' populism to indicate the values that this populism pursues.

By acknowledging the crucial role played by the democratic discourse in the political imaginary of our societies and by establishing, around democracy as the hegemonic signifier, a chain of equivalence among the manifold struggles against subordination, a left populist strategy resonates with the aspirations of many people. In the next few years, I argue, the central axis of the political conflict will be between right-wing populism and left-wing populism. And as a result, it is through the construction of a 'people', a collective will that results from the mobilization of common affects in defence of equality and social justice, that it will be possible to combat the xenophobic policies promoted by right-wing populism.

In recreating political frontiers, the 'populist moment' points to a 'return of the political' after years of postpolitics. This return may open the way for authoritarian solutions – through regimes that weaken liberal-democratic institutions – but it can also lead to a reaffirmation and extension of democratic values. Everything will depend on which political forces will succeed in hegemonizing the current democratic demands and the kind of populism that emerges victorious from the struggle against post-politics.

I

The Populist Moment

I would like to make clear at the outset that my aim is not to add another contribution to the already plethoric field of 'populism studies' and I have no intention to enter the sterile academic debate about the 'true nature' of populism. This book is meant to be a political intervention and it openly acknowledges its partisan nature. I will define what I understand by 'left populism' and argue that in the present conjuncture it provides the adequate strategy to recover and deepen the ideals of equality and popular sovereignty that are constitutive of a democratic politics.

As a political theorist, my mode of theorizing takes its bearing from Machiavelli, who, as Althusser reminded us, always situated himself 'in the conjuncture' instead of reflecting 'over the conjuncture'. Following Machiavelli's example, I will inscribe my reflection in a particular conjuncture, looking for what he called the *verita effetuale de la cosa* (the effectual truth of the thing) of the 'populist moment' we are currently witnessing in Western European countries. I limit my analysis to Western Europe because, although the question of populism is, no doubt, also relevant in Eastern Europe, those countries necessitate a special analysis. They are marked by their specific history under communism and their political culture presents different features. This is also the case with the various forms of Latin American populism. While there are 'family resemblances' between the various populisms, they correspond to characteristic conjunctures and they need to be apprehended according to their various contexts. Hopefully, my reflections on the Western European conjuncture will provide some useful insights to address other populist situations.

Even if my objective is a political one, a significant part of my reflections will be of a theoretical nature because the left populist strategy that I am going to defend is informed by an anti-essentialist theoretical approach that asserts that society is always divided and discursively constructed through hegemonic practices. Many criticisms addressed to 'left populism' are based on a lack of understanding of this approach and this is why it is important to make it explicit here. I will refer to the central tenets of the anti-essentialist approach at several points in my argument and further clarifications will be provided in a theoretical appendix at the end of the book.

To dispel any possible confusion, I will begin by specifying what I understand by 'populism'. Discarding the derogatory meaning of that term that has been imposed by the media to disqualify all those who oppose the status quo, I will follow the analytical approach developed by Ernesto Laclau that permits addressing the question of populism in a way that I find particularly fruitful.

In his book *On Populist Reason*, Laclau defines populism as a discursive strategy of constructing a political frontier dividing society into two camps and calling for the mobilization of the 'underdog' against 'those in power'.[1] It is not an ideology and cannot be attributed a specific programmatic content. Nor is it a political regime. It is a way of doing politics that can take various ideological forms according to both time and place, and is compatible with a variety of institutional frameworks. We can speak of a 'populist moment' when, under the pressure of political or socioeconomic transformations, the dominant hegemony is being destabilized by the multiplication of unsatisfied demands. In such situations, the existing institutions fail to secure the allegiance of the people as they attempt to defend the existing order. As a result, the historical bloc that provides the social basis of a hegemonic formation is being disarticulated and the possibility arises of constructing a new subject of collective action – the people – capable of reconfiguring a social order experienced as unjust.

This, I contend, is precisely what characterizes our present conjuncture and this is why it is apposite to call it a 'populist moment'. This populist moment signals the crisis of the neoliberal hegemonic formation that was progressively implemented in Western Europe through the 1980s. This neoliberal hegemonic formation replaced the social-democratic Keynesian welfare state that, in the thirty years after the end of the Second World War, provided the principal socioeconomic model in the democratic countries in Western Europe. The core of this new hegemonic formation is constituted by a set of political-economic practices aimed at imposing the rule of the

1 Ernesto Laclau, *On Populist Reason* (New York and London: Verso, 2005).

market – deregulation, privatization, fiscal austerity – and limiting the role of the state to the protection of private property rights, free markets and free trade. Neoliberalism is the term currently used to refer to this new hegemonic formation which, far from being limited to the economic domain, also connotes a whole conception of society and of the individual grounded on a philosophy of possessive individualism.

This model, implemented in various countries from the 1980s onwards, did not face any significant challenge until the financial crisis of 2008, when it began to seriously show its limits. This crisis, initiated in 2007 in the US with the collapse of the subprime mortgage market, developed into a full-blown international banking crisis with the failure of the investment bank Lehman Brothers the following year. Massive bailouts of financial institutions had to be initiated to impede the breakdown of the world financial system. The global economic downturn that followed deeply affected several European economies and provoked a European debt crisis. In order to deal with this crisis, policies of austerity were implemented in most European countries, with drastic effects, particularly in the Southern countries.

On the occasion of the economic crisis, a series of contradictions condensed, leading to what Gramsci calls an *interregnum*: a period of crisis during which several tenets of the consensus established around a hegemonic project are challenged. A solution to the crisis is not yet in sight and this characterizes the 'populist moment' in which we find ourselves today. The 'populist moment', therefore, is the expression of a variety of resistances to the political and economic transformations seen during the years of neoliberal hegemony. These transformations have led to a situation that we could call 'post-democracy' to indicate the erosion of the two pillars of the democratic ideal: equality and popular sovereignty. I will explain in a moment how such an erosion took place but before that, it is worth examining what is meant by 'post-democracy'.

'Post-democracy', first proposed by Colin Crouch, signals the decline in the role of parliaments and the loss of sovereignty that is the consequence of neoliberal globalization. According to Crouch:

> The fundamental cause of democratic decline in contemporary politics is the major imbalance now developing between the role of corporate interests and those of virtually all other groups. Taken alongside the inevitable entropy of democracy, this is leading to politics once again becoming an affair of closed elites, as it was in pre-democratic times.[2]

Jacques Rancière also uses this term, which he defines in the following way:

> Post-democracy is the government practice and conceptual legitimization of a democracy *after* the demos, a democracy that has eliminated the appearance, miscount, and dispute of the people and is thereby reducible to the sole interplay of state mechanisms and combinations of social energies and interests.[3]

2 Colin Crouch, *Post-Democracy* (Cambridge, UK: Polity, 2004), p. 104.
3 Jacques Rancière, *Disagreement: Politics and Philosophy*, trans. Julie Rose (Minneapolis: University of Minnesota Press, 1999), p. 102.

While not disagreeing with either definition, my use of the term is somewhat different because, through a reflection on the nature of liberal democracy, I aim to bring to the fore a different feature of neoliberalism. As is well known, etymologically speaking, 'democracy' comes from the Greek *demos/kratos*, which means 'the power of the people'. When we speak of 'democracy' in Europe, we refer, however, to a specific model: the Western model that results from the inscription of the democratic principle in a particular historical context. This model has received a variety of names: representative democracy, constitutional democracy, liberal democracy, pluralist democracy.

In all cases what is in question is a political regime characterized by the articulation of two different traditions. On the one hand, the tradition of political liberalism: the rule of law, the separation of powers and the defence of individual freedom; on the other hand, the democratic tradition, whose central ideas are equality and popular sovereignty. There is no necessary relationship between these two traditions but only a contingent historical articulation that, as CB Macpherson has shown, took place through the joint struggles of the liberals and the democrats against absolutist regimes.[4]

Some authors, like Carl Schmitt, affirm that this articulation produced an unviable regime because liberalism denies democracy and democracy denies liberalism. Others, following Jürgen Habermas, maintain the 'co-originality' of the principles of freedom and equality. Schmitt is certainly right in pointing out the existence of a conflict between the liberal 'grammar,' which postulates

4   CB Macpherson, *The Life and Times of Liberal Democracy* (Oxford: Oxford University Press, 1977).

universality and the reference to 'humanity', and the 'grammar' of democratic equality, which requires the construction of a people and a frontier between a 'we' and a 'they'. But I think he is mistaken in presenting that conflict as a contradiction that must inevitably lead a pluralistic liberal democracy to self-destruction.

In *The Democratic Paradox*, I conceived the articulation of these two traditions – indeed, ultimately irreconcilable – on the mode of a paradoxical configuration, as the *locus* of a *tension* that defines the originality of liberal democracy as a *politeia,* a form of political community, that guarantees its pluralistic character.[5] The democratic logic of constructing a people and defending egalitarian practices is necessary to define a *demos* and to subvert the tendency of liberal discourse to abstract universalism. But its articulation with liberal logic allows us to challenge the forms of exclusion that are inherent in the political practices of determining the people that will govern.

Democratic liberal politics consists of a constant process of negotiation through different hegemonic configurations of this constitutive tension. This tension, expressed in political terms along the frontier between right and left, can only be stabilized temporarily through pragmatic negotiations between political forces. These negotiations always establish the hegemony of one of them over the other. Revisiting the history of liberal democracy, we find that on some occasions the liberal logic prevailed, while in others it was the democratic. Nonetheless the two logics remained in force, and the possibility of an 'agonistic' negotiation between right and

5 Chantal Mouffe, *The Democratic Paradox* (New York and London: Verso, 2000).

left, which is specific to the liberal-democratic regime, always remained active.

The previous considerations only concern liberal democracy envisaged as a political regime, but it is evident that those political institutions never exist independently of their inscription in an economic system. In the case of neoliberalism, for instance, we are dealing with a social formation that articulates a particular form of liberal democracy with financial capitalism. Although this articulation needs to be taken into account when studying a specific social formation, it is possible, at the analytical level, to examine the evolution of the liberal-democratic regime as a political form of society, so as to bring to the fore some of its characteristics.

The current situation can be described as 'post-democracy' because in recent years, as a consequence of neoliberal hegemony, the agonistic tension between the liberal and the democratic principles, which is constitutive of liberal democracy, has been eliminated. With the demise of the democratic values of equality and popular sovereignty, the agonistic spaces where different projects of society could confront each other have disappeared and citizens have been deprived of the possibility of exercising their democratic rights. To be sure, 'democracy' is still spoken of, but it has been reduced to its liberal component and it only signifies the presence of free elections and the defence of human rights. What has become increasingly central is economic liberalism with its defence of the free market and many aspects of political liberalism have been relegated to second place, if not simply eliminated. This is what I mean by 'post-democracy'.

In the political arena, the evolution towards postdemocracy was made manifest through what I proposed in *On the Political* to call 'post-politics', which blurs the political frontier between the right and the left.[6] Under the pretext of the 'modernization' imposed by globalization, social-democratic parties have accepted the *diktats* of financial capitalism and the limits they imposed to state interventions and their redistributive policies.

As a result the role of parliaments and institutions that allow citizens to influence political decisions has been drastically reduced. Elections no longer offer any opportunity to decide on real alternatives through the traditional 'parties of government'. The only thing that post-politics allows is a bipartisan alternation of power between centre-right and centre-left parties. All those who oppose the 'consensus in the centre' and the dogma that there is no alternative to neoliberal globalization are presented as 'extremists' or disqualified as 'populists'.

Politics therefore has become a mere issue of managing the established order, a domain reserved for experts, and popular sovereignty has been declared obsolete. One of the fundamental symbolic pillars of the democratic ideal – the power of the people – has been undermined because post-politics eliminates the possibility of an agonistic struggle between different projects of society which is the very condition for the exercise of popular sovereignty.

Next to post-politics, there is another development that needs to be taken into account when understanding the causes of the post-democratic condition: the growing 'oligarchization' of Western European societies. Changes at the political level have taken place in the context of a new mode of regulation of capitalism, where financial

6   Chantal Mouffe, *On the Political* (Abingdon, UK: Routledge, 2005).

capital occupies a central place. With the financialization of the economy, there was a great expansion of the financial sector at the expense of the productive economy. This explains the exponential increase in inequalities we have witnessed in recent years.

Privatization and deregulation policies contributed to a drastic deterioration in the conditions of the workers. Under the combined effects of deindustrialization, the promotion of technological changes and processes of relocation of industries to countries where labour was cheaper, many jobs were lost.

With the effects of the austerity policies that were imposed after the 2008 crisis, this situation also affects a large part of the middle class, which has entered into a process of pauperization and precarization. As a result of this process of oligarchization, the other pillar of the democratic ideal – the defence of equality – has also been eliminated from the liberal-democratic discourse. What now rules is an individualistic liberal vision that celebrates consumer society and the freedom that the markets offer.

It is in the post-democratic context of the erosion of the democratic ideals of popular sovereignty and equality that the 'populist moment' should be apprehended. It is characterized by the emergence of manifold resistances against a politico-economic system that is increasingly perceived as being controlled by privileged elites who are deaf to the demands of the other groups in society. At the beginning, most of the political resistances against the post-democratic consensus came from the right. In the 1990s, right-wing populist parties like the FPÖ in Austria and the Front National in France began to present themselves as aiming to give back to 'the people' the voice of which they had been deprived by the elites. By drawing a frontier between the 'people' and the 'political establishment', they were able to translate into a nationalistic vocabulary the demands of the popular sectors who felt excluded from the dominant consensus.

This is, for instance, how Jörg Haider transformed the Freedom Party of Austria into a protest party against the 'grand coalition'. By mobilizing the themes of popular sovereignty, he managed to articulate the growing resistances to the way the country was governed by a coalition of elites that impeded a real democratic debate.[7]

The political panorama, which had already shown signs of left radicalization with a variety of anti-globalization movements, changed significantly in 2011. When austerity policies began to affect the living conditions of broad sectors of the population, important popular protests took place in several European countries and the post-political consensus began to unravel. In Greece the Aganakitsmenoi and in Spain the Indignados of the M15 occupied central squares, calling for 'Democracy Now!' They were followed by the Occupy movement which, born in the US, had manifestations in various cities in Europe, particularly in London and Frankfurt. More recently, Nuit Debout in France in 2016 was the expression of those forms of protest referred to as 'movements of the squares'.

Those protests were the signal of a political awakening after years of relative apathy. However, the refusal of those horizontalist movements to engage with the political institutions limited their impact. And without any

7 In 'The "End of Politics" and the Challenge of Right-Wing Populism', I analyzed the growth of the Freedom Party of Austria under Jörg Haider. See Francisco Panizza, ed., *Populism and the Mirror of Democracy* (New York and London: Verso, 2005), pp. 50–71.

form of articulation with institutional politics, they soon began to lose their dynamics. Although such protest movements have certainly played a role in the transformation of political consciousness, it is only when they have been followed by structured political movements, ready to engage with political institutions, that significant results have been achieved.

It is in Greece and in Spain where we witnessed the first political movements implementing a form of populism aimed at the recovery and deepening of democracy. In Greece, Syriza – a united social front born of a coalition of different left movements around Synaspismos, the former Eurocommunist party – signalled the emergence of a new type of radical party whose objective was to challenge neoliberal hegemony through parliamentary politics. By establishing a synergy between social movements and party politics, Syriza was able to articulate in a collective will a variety of democratic demands and this allowed it to come to power in January 2015.

Unfortunately, Syriza has not been able to implement its anti-austerity programme because of the brutal response of the European Union that reacted with a 'financial coup' and forced the party to accept the *diktats* of the Troika. This does not invalidate the populist strategy that allowed it to come to power, but it certainly raises important issues with respect to the limitations that the membership of the European Union imposes on the possibility of carrying out policies that challenge neoliberalism.

In Spain the meteoric rise of Podemos in 2014 was due to the capacity of a group of young intellectuals to take advantage of the terrain created by the Indignados. This led to the creation of a party movement aiming at breaking the stalemate of the consensual politics established through the transition to democracy whose exhaustion had become evident. The Podemos strategy of creating a popular collective will by constructing a frontier between the establishment elites (la 'casta') and the 'people' has not yet managed to dislodge the right-wing Partido Popular from the government, but Podemos members have been able to enter Parliament, where they deposed an important group of MPs. Since then, they have represented an important force in Spanish politics and have profoundly transformed the Spanish political landscape.

Similar developments have taken place in other countries: in Germany with Die Linke, in Portugal with the Bloco de Esquerda and in France with La France Insoumise of Jean-Luc Mélenchon, which in June 2017, one year after its creation, gained seventeen MPs in Parliament and now represents the main opposition to the government of Emmanuel Macron. Finally, the unexpected good result of the British Labour Party under the leadership of Jeremy Corbyn, also in June 2017, is another sign of a new form of radicalism emerging in several European countries.

The social-democratic parties, who in many countries have played an important role in the implementation of neoliberal policies, are unable to grasp the nature of the populist moment and to face the challenge that it represents. Prisoners of their post-political dogmas, and reluctant to admit their mistakes, they cannot recognize that many of the demands articulated by right-wing populist parties are democratic demands, to which a progressive answer must be given. Many of those demands come from the groups who are the main losers of neoliberal globalization, and they cannot be satisfied within the neoliberal project.

Classifying right-wing populist parties as 'extreme-right' or 'neofascist' and attributing their appeal to lack of education is of course especially convenient for the forces of the centre-left. It is an easy way to disqualify them, without recognizing the centre-left's own responsibility in such an emergence. By establishing a 'moral' frontier so as to exclude the 'extremists' from the democratic debate, the 'good democrats' believe that they can stop the rise of 'irrational' passions. Such a strategy of demonization of the 'enemies' of the bipartisan consensus can be morally comforting, but it is politically disempowering.

To stop the rise of right-wing populist parties, it is necessary to design a properly political answer through a left populist movement that will federate all the democratic struggles against post-democracy. Instead of excluding *a priori* the voters of right-wing populist parties as necessarily moved by atavistic passions, condemning them to remain prisoners of those passions forever, it is necessary to recognize the democratic nucleus at the origin of many of their demands.

A left populist approach should try to provide a different vocabulary in order to orientate those demands towards more egalitarian objectives. This does not mean condoning the politics of right-wing populist parties, but refusing to attribute to their voters the responsibility for the way their demands are articulated. I do not deny that there are people who feel perfectly at home with those reactionary values, but I am convinced there are others who are attracted to those parties because they feel they are the only ones that care about their problems. I believe that, if a different language is made available, many people might experience their situation in a different way and join the progressive struggle.

There are already several examples that such a strategy can work. For instance, in the 2017 legislative elections in France, Jean-Luc Mélenchon and other candidates of La France Insoumise such as François Ruffin were able to win the support of voters who had previously voted for Marine Le Pen. Arguing with people who, under the influence of the Front National, had been led to see immigrants as responsible for their deprivation, activists were able to make such voters alter their views. Their sentiment of being left behind and their desire for democratic recognition, previously expressed in xenophobic language, could be formulated in a different vocabulary and directed towards another adversary. Something similar happened in Britain in the June 2017 elections where 16 per cent of voters of the right-wing populist UKIP voted for Jeremy Corbyn.

Now that the anti-establishment discourse also comes from the progressive side, and that political forces on the left are drawing a frontier between the 'people' and the 'oligarchy', we are really in the midst of a 'populist moment'. What is at stake in this moment, therefore, is how the resistances to post-democracy are going to be articulated and how 'the people' is going to be constructed. There are many ways in which this can be done. And not all populist constructions of the political frontier have egalitarian objectives, even when the rejection of the existing system is made in the name of giving power back to the people.

Both types of populism aim to federate unsatisfied demands, but they do it in very different ways. The difference lies in the composition of the 'we' and in how the adversary, the 'they,' is defined.

Right-wing populism claims that it will bring back popular sovereignty and restore democracy, but this sovereignty is understood as 'national sovereignty' and reserved for those deemed to be true 'nationals'. Right-wing populists do not address the demand for equality and they construct a 'people' that excludes numerous categories, usually immigrants, seen as a threat to the identity and the prosperity of the nation. It is worth signalling that, although right-wing populism articulates many resistances against post-democracy, it does not necessarily present the adversary of the people as being constituted by the forces of neoliberalism. It would there-fore be a mistake to identify their opposition to post-democracy with a rejection of neoliberalism. Their victory could lead to nationalistic authoritarian forms of neolib-eralism that, in the name of recovering democracy, in fact drastically restrict it.

Left populism on the contrary wants to recover democ-racy to deepen and extend it. A left populist strategy aims at federating the democratic demands into a collective will to construct a 'we', a 'people' confronting a common adversary: the oligarchy. This requires the establishment of a chain of equivalence among the demands of the workers, the immigrants and the precarious middle class, as well as other democratic demands, such as those of the LGBT community. The objective of such a chain is the creation of a new hegemony that will permit the radicali-zation of democracy.

2
Learning from Thatcherism

The 'populist moment' that we are witnessing throughout Western Europe offers the opportunity to bring about an alternative to the neoliberal hegemonic formation which is now in crisis. The crucial question is how to operate this transition. Are there examples from which we could learn to imagine which steps to follow? Perhaps scrutinizing the conditions in which the neoliberal model became hegemonic in Western Europe could provide us with some clues about how a hegemonic transformation can take place. This is the conjuncture that we examined in *Hegemony and Socialist Strategy* and it might therefore be relevant to revisit some of its analyses.

The book was written in London at the time of the crisis of the postwar consensus established between Labour and the Tories around the Keynesian welfare state. And it was principally within this British context that we developed our reflections on the future of left politics. Yet I believe that their pertinence is not limited to Britain. As has been pointed out by Wolfgang Streeck:

The structure of the post-war settlement between labour and capital was fundamentally the same across the otherwise widely different countries where democratic capitalism had come to be instituted. It included an expanding welfare state, the right of workers to free collective bargaining and a political guarantee of full employment, underwritten by governments making extensive use of the Keynesian economic toolkit.[1]

To apprehend the nature of the Keynesian welfare state as a hegemonic formation, it is necessary to acknowledge that, although it played a crucial role in subordinating the reproduction of the labour force to the needs of capital, it also laid the conditions for the emergence of a new type of social rights and profoundly transformed democratic common sense, giving legitimacy to a set of demands for economic equality. In several countries, the strength of the trade unions allowed the consolidation of social rights. Meanwhile, the growth of inequality was kept in check, the workers made substantial gains, and important democratic advances were achieved during these years. As a compromise between capital and labour, it allowed a sort of uneasy coexistence between capitalism and democracy.

However, during the first half of the 1970s, economic slowdown and rising inflation began to show the limits of the Keynesian compromise. Under the effects of the 1973 oil crisis, the economy suffered, profits declined and the postwar social-democratic settlement began to crumble. In Britain, faced with a fiscal crisis, the Labour Party in power had to use the state to discipline the working

1   Wolfgang Streeck, 'The Crises of Democratic Capitalism', *New Left Review* 71 (September/October 2011), 10.

classes, leading to growing disaffection. By the mid-70s, the postwar social-democratic model was in serious trouble and it began to suffer from a 'legitimation crisis'.

Economic factors are not sufficient, however, to fully grasp the crisis of the social-democratic model. We also need to take into account other factors, particularly the emergence in the 1960s of what have been called 'the new social movements'. This term was used at the time to refer to very diverse struggles: urban, ecological, anti-authoritarian, anti-institutional, feminist, anti-racist, ethnic, regional and that of sexual minorities. The political polarization created around those new democratic demands, jointly with a wave of labour militancy, provoked a reaction from conservatives, who claimed that the multiplication of the struggles for equality had led Western societies to the edge of the 'egalitarian precipice'. When the economic recession came after 1973, the right decided that the time had come to stop the expansion of the democratic imaginary. They planned to counter this egalitarian movement and to restore the profits that had been kept in check by the power of the unions. In his report to the Trilateral Commission in 1975, Samuel Huntington declared that the struggles in the 60s for greater equality and participation had produced a 'democratic surge' that had made society 'ungovernable'. He concluded that 'the strength of the democratic ideal poses a problem for the governability of democracy.'[2]

At the time that we were writing our book, Margaret Thatcher had just won the elections but the outcome of the crisis was still unclear. This is how we viewed the situation:

2 Samuel Huntington, 'The Democratic Distemper', in *The American Commonwealth*, ed. Nathan Glazer and Irving Kristol (New York: Basic Books, 1976), p. 37.

> It cannot be doubted that the proliferation of new antagonisms and of 'new rights' is leading to a crisis of the hegemonic formation of the post-war period. But the form in which this crisis will be overcome is far from being predetermined, as the manner in which rights will be defined and the forms which struggle against subordination will adopt are not unequivocally established.[3]

We claimed that, to counter the offensive of the right, it was crucial for Labour to expand its social basis by acknowledging the shortcomings of its corporatist politics and to incorporate the critics made by the new social movements, whose democratic demands it was essential to articulate alongside those of the working class. The objective was to constitute a new historical bloc around a socialist project redefined in terms of the 'radicalization of democracy'. We were convinced that only a hegemonic project aiming at the extension of the democratic principles of liberty and equality to a wider set of social relations could offer a progressive outcome to the crisis.

Alas, the Labour Party, prisoner of its economistic and essentialist vision, was unable to grasp the need for a hegemonic politics and it clung to an old-fashioned defence of its traditional positions. It was thereby unable to resist the assault of the forces opposed to the Keynesian model and this opened the way for the cultural and ideological victory of the neoliberal project.

Margaret Thatcher's objective when she became prime minister in 1979 was to break the postwar consensus

3   Ernesto Laclau and Chantal Mouffe, *Hegemony and Socialist Strategy: Towards a Radical Democratic Politics*, paperback edition (New York and London: Verso, 2014), p. 152.

between Tories and Labour, which she claimed to be the cause of British stagnation. Contrary to the Labour Party, she was well aware of the partisan nature of politics and the importance of the hegemonic struggle. Her strategy was clearly a populist one. It consisted in drawing a political frontier between, on one side, the 'forces of the establishment', identified with the oppressive state bureaucrats, the trade unions and those who benefited from state handouts, and, on the other, the industrious 'people' who were the victims of the various bureaucratic forces and their different allies.

Her main target was the trade unions whose power she decided to destroy; she engaged in a frontal confrontation with the National Union of Mineworkers led by Arthur Scargill, whom she declared to be 'the enemy within'. The miners' strike (1984–5), the most bitter industrial dispute in Britain's history, was a turning point in her trajectory. It ended with a decisive victory for the government that was thereafter in a position to impose its conditions on a weakened trade union movement and to consolidate its economically liberal programme.

In a moment when the postwar Keynesian consensus was cracking, Margaret Thatcher intervened in order to forcefully challenge the status quo. By erecting a political frontier, she was able to disarticulate the key elements of the social-democratic hegemony and to establish a new hegemonic order based on popular consent. This is something that Labour politicians with their essentialist view of politics could not grasp. Instead of developing a counter-hegemonic offensive, they were convinced that the increase in the unemployment level caused by neoliberal policies and the worsening of the conditions of the workers would soon put them back in government. They were passively expecting the deterioration of the economic conditions to work in their favour without realizing that, in the meantime, Thatcher was consolidating her neoliberal revolution.

Analyzing the hegemonic strategy that he called 'Thatcherism' and defined as 'authoritarian populism', Stuart Hall noted that 'Thatcherite populism . . . combines the resonant themes of organic Toryism – nation, family, duty, authority, standards, traditionalism – with the aggressive themes of a revived neoliberalism – self-interest, competitive individualism, anti-statism.'[4] Thatcher's success in implementing neoliberal policies in Britain was made possible by her capacity to capitalize on the resistances to the collectivist and bureaucratic way in which the welfare state had been implemented.

Thatcher was able to get the support of many sectors for her neoliberal project because they were attracted by her celebration of individual freedom and her promise to liberate them from the oppressive power of the state. Such a discourse resonated, even with the beneficiaries of state intervention, as they resented the bureaucratic way in which those benefits were often distributed. By opposing the interests of some categories of workers to those of the feminists and the immigrants, presented as being responsible for stealing their jobs, she managed to win to her side important sectors of the working class.

In her onslaught against the social-democratic hegemony, Margaret Thatcher intervened on several fronts – economic, political and ideological – to discursively reconfigure what

4   Stuart Hall, 'Learning from Thatcherism', in *The Hard Road to Renewal* (New York and London: Verso, 1988), p. 271.'Learning from Thatcherism' is the title of the conclusion.

was up to that moment considered 'common sense' and combat its social-democratic values. The main objective was to sever the link that had been established between liberalism and democracy through which, as CB Macpherson argued, liberalism had been 'democratized'.

Friedrich Hayek, Thatcher's favourite philosopher, insisted on the need to reaffirm the 'true' nature of liberalism as the doctrine that seeks to reduce the powers of the state to a minimum in order to maximize the central political objective: individual liberty. This was the notion that he defined negatively as 'that condition of men in which coercion of some by others is reduced as much as possible in society'.[5]

Another move in this ideological strategy was to foster the re-signification of 'democracy', subordinating it to 'freedom'. According to Hayek, the idea of democracy is secondary to the idea of individual liberty, so that a defence of economic liberty and private property replaces a defence of equality as the privileged value in a liberal society. For him, 'democracy is essentially a means, a utilitarian device for safeguarding internal peace and individual freedom.'[6] He was adamant that if a conflict were to arise between democracy and freedom, priority should be given to freedom and democracy should be sacrificed. In his later years, he even went to the extreme of suggesting the abolition of democracy.

With a discourse opposing the good, responsible 'taxpayers' to the bureaucratic elites which were restraining the taxpayers' liberty through abusive use of state

5 Friedrich Hayek, *The Constitution of Liberty* (Chicago: University of Chicago Press, 1960), p. 11.

6 Friedrich Hayek, *The Road to Serfdom* (London: Routledge, 1944), p. 52.

power, Thatcher succeeded in consolidating a historical bloc around her neoliberal vision and profoundly transforming the configuration of social and economic forces. At some point, however, her politics was perceived as too divisive by the Tories and, after having won three elections, when the implementation of the poll tax in 1989 led to outbreaks of street violence, they forced her to resign in 1990.

By that time, however, Margaret Thatcher had secured her neoliberal revolution and when she left the government, the neoliberal vision had become so deeply ingrained in the common sense that, when Labour came back to power in 1997 with Tony Blair, it did not even try to challenge the neoliberal hegemony. Indeed, as Hall showed, one finds in the discourse of New Labour all the key Thatcherite discursive figures:

> the 'taxpayer' (hard-working man, over-taxed to fund the welfare 'scrounger') and the 'customer' (fortunate housewife, 'free' to exercise limited choice in the marketplace, for whom the 'choice agenda' and personalised delivery were specifically designed). No-one ever thinks either could also be a citizen who needs or relies on public services.[7]

No wonder that when asked in later years what had been her greatest achievement, Margaret Thatcher replied. 'Tony Blair and New Labour. We forced our opponents to change their minds.'

---

7   Stuart Hall, 'The Neoliberal Revolution', in *The Neoliberal Crisis*, ed. Sally Davison and Katharine Harris (London: Lawrence & Wishart, 2015), p. 25.

What was in fact a capitulation to neoliberalism was theorized by the people around 'New Labour' as a 'third way', a form of politics 'beyond left and right' and presented as the most advanced conception of 'progressive politics'. Now that the neoliberal hegemonic formation had been firmly established, the need for a political frontier between 'we' and 'they' was deemed to belong to an obsolete model of politics and the 'consensus at the centre' was celebrated as a step towards a mature form of democracy in which antagonism had been overcome. This consensual 'third way' model was later adopted as the credo of the main European social-democratic and socialist parties. Following the collapse of the Soviet model, this model became the only acceptable vision for a democratic left, signalling the full transformation of social democracy into social liberalism. This created the terrain for the reign of the post-politics that provided the conditions for the consolidation of neoliberal hegemony in Western Europe.

This consolidation of neoliberal hegemony was accompanied by some significant changes. While the ideology of Thatcherism was a combination of conservative themes of organic Toryism with neoliberal economic practices, the neoliberalism that became hegemonic in later years moved away from the traditional conservative ideology. To respond to the transformation in the mode of regulation of capitalism linked to the transition from Fordism to post-Fordism, the neoliberal hegemonic formation incorporated several themes of the counterculture. In their book *The New Spirit of Capitalism*, Luc Boltanski and Eve Chiapello bring to light the way in which, faced with the challenge represented by the new movements, capitalists managed to use the demands for autonomy of those movements, harnessing them in the development of the post-Fordist networked economy and transforming them into new forms of control.[8] Several forms of 'artistic critique', the term they use to refer to the aesthetic strategies of the counterculture including the search for authenticity, the ideal of self-management and the anti-hierarchical exigency, were used to promote the conditions required by the new mode of capitalist regulation, replacing the disciplinary framework characteristic of the Fordist period. This created favourable conditions to co-opt and neutralize many of the demands of the new social movements, using them to liberalize labour and promote a selfish individualism.

Several theorists on the left have been very critical of Boltanski and Chiapello, accusing them of presenting the countercultural movements as being responsible for the victory of neoliberal values. Such interpretation is based on a misunderstanding of their approach whose interest, from a hegemonic perspective, as I pointed out in *Agonistics*, allows us to visualize the transition from Fordism to post-Fordism in terms of what Gramsci calls 'hegemony through neutralization' or 'passive revolution'.[9] By that, he refers to a situation where demands that challenge the hegemonic order are recuperated by the existing system, satisfying them in a way that neutralizes their subversive potential. Thanks to a process of 'detournement' of the discourses and practices of the countercultural critique, capital was able to resist the challenge that those demands could have represented to its legitimacy and to consolidate its supremacy.

8   Luc Boltanski and Eve Chiapello, *The New Spirit of Capitalism* (London and New York: Verso, 2005).
9   Chantal Mouffe, *Agonistics: Thinking the World Politically* (London and New York: Verso, 2013).

This solution did work for a time but, after years of undisputed hegemony, neoliberalism has now entered into crisis, and the possibility has arisen for the left to build a different hegemonic order. This is an opportunity that cannot be missed and in envisaging how to intervene in this conjuncture, I propose to learn from Thatcher's strategy. This might seem a provocation, but I am not the first one to make such a proposal – although in a different context, this was also what Stuart Hall suggested in his book *The Hard Road to Renewal*, where he underlined that, contrary to Labour, Thatcher had been able to develop a hegemonic political project, putting in play a range of different social and economic strategies without neglecting the ideological dimension.[10]

The current crisis of the neoliberal hegemonic formation offers the possibility of intervening to establish a different order. We should follow Thatcher's route, adopting a populist strategy, but this time with a progressive objective, intervening on a multiplicity of fronts to build a new hegemony aiming at recovering and deepening democracy. The populist moment calls for such a type of intervention.

While the crisis of neoliberalism provides the opportunity to construct a new hegemonic order, there is no guarantee that this new order will bring about significant democratic advances and it might even be of an authoritarian nature. This is why it is crucial for the left not to repeat the mistakes of the past. It is imperative that it relinquish the essentialist conception of politics that prevents it from grasping its hegemonic dimension.

10   Stuart Hall, 'Learning from Thatcherism', in *The Hard Road to Renewal* (New York and London: Verso, 1988), p. 271. 'Learning from Thatcherism' is the title of the conclusion.

What is urgently needed is a left populist strategy aimed at the construction of a 'people', combining the variety of democratic resistances against post-democracy in order to establish a more democratic hegemonic formation. This will necessitate a far-reaching transformation of the existing relations of power and the creation of new democratic practices, but I contend that it does not require a 'revolutionary' break with the liberal-democratic regime. No doubt there are those on the left who will claim that such an eventuality is unviable. But I consider that the experience of Thatcherism shows that, in European societies, it is possible to bring about a transformation of the existing hegemonic order without destroying liberal-democratic institutions.

To learn from Thatcherism means realizing that in the present conjuncture, the decisive move is to establish a political frontier that breaks with the post-political consensus between centre-right and centre-left. Without defining an adversary, no hegemonic offensive can be launched. However, this is precisely the step that social-democratic parties, converted to neoliberalism, are unable to make. This is because they believe that democracy should aim at reaching consensus and that it is possible to have a politics without an adversary.

A left populist strategy needs to challenge such a view, but the relations of forces are clearly less favourable today than in the conjuncture that we examined in *Hegemony and Socialist Strategy*. During the years of neoliberal hegemony, many of the social-democratic advances have been dismantled. And we find ourselves in the paradoxical situation of having to defend various welfare state institutions that we criticized earlier for not being radical enough.

At the time of the crisis of the postwar consensus, social democracy, although weakened by the growth of inflation and the economic recession, had not yet been ideologically defeated. And, had it been able to design an adequate hegemonic strategy, it might possibly have managed to defend its social advances. Many democratic values that were central elements of the social-democratic common sense were still in force and it was possible to envisage the project of the left in terms of their radicalization. Obviously this is no longer the case, and there is no way that we could think of 'radicalizing' neoliberalism. Nowadays, before being able to radicalize democracy, it is first necessary to recover it.

The actual conjuncture calls for a rupture with the existing hegemonic formation, and this is something that social liberal parties are unable to acknowledge. Those parties have become too deeply integrated within the neoliberal hegemonic formation and their reformist discourse does not allow them to draw a political frontier and to visualize an alternative vision. For such parties to be able to offer a solution to the crisis requires a profound transformation of their identity and their strategy.

Since the collapse of the Soviet model, many sectors of the left are unable to visualize an alternative to the liberal view of politics other than the revolutionary one that they have discarded. Their recognition that the 'friend/enemy' model of politics is incompatible with pluralist democracy and that liberal democracy is not an enemy to be destroyed is to be applauded. But it has led them to negate the existence of antagonisms altogether and to accept the liberal conception that reduces politics to a competition among elites in a neutral terrain. The inability to envisage a hegemonic strategy is, I believe, the main shortcoming of social-democratic parties. This is what impedes them from understanding the possibility of an adversarial, agonistic politics oriented towards the establishment of a different hegemonic order within the liberal-democratic framework.

Fortunately there are some exceptions, as evidenced by the evolution of the British Labour Party that, under the leadership of Jeremy Corbyn, is implementing what corresponds to a left populist strategy. Contrary to the sectors of Labour who want to maintain the consensual model instigated by Tony Blair, Corbyn's followers and the Momentum movement have been promoting the establishment of a political frontier between the people and the establishment. It is very telling that for the recent electoral campaign, they used the Blairite slogan 'For the many, not the few', but re-signified it in an agonistic way as constructing a political frontier between 'we' and 'they'.

By making a clear break with the post-politics of the Blair years, and by designing a radical programme, Corbyn's re-politicized Labour Party has been able to win back many disillusioned voters and to attract a huge following among young people. This testifies to the capacity of left populism to give a new impulse to democratic politics.

The significant increase in the membership of the Labour Party under Corbyn also indicates that, contrary to what so many political scientists are claiming, the 'form' party has not become obsolete and it can be reactivated. Indeed, the Labour Party with almost 600,000 members is now the biggest European left-wing party. This shows that the disaffection experienced by political parties in recent years was a consequence of the post-political lack of alternative that was offered to citizens, and that this situation is reversed when they are given the possibility of identifying with a programme of radicalization of democracy.

3

Radicalizing Democracy

What does it mean to radicalize democracy? This is something that I need to clarify because there are many conceptions of radical democracy and serious misunderstandings have arisen with respect to the 'radical and plural democracy' that was defended in *Hegemony and Socialist Strategy*. Some people believed that we were calling for a total rupture with liberal democracy and for the creation of a completely new regime. In fact, what we were advocating was a 'radicalization' of the ethico-political principles of liberal-democratic regime, 'liberty and equality for all'.

An important dimension of this project was to question the belief held by some people on the left that to move towards a more just society, it was necessary to relinquish liberal-democratic institutions and to build a completely new *politeia*, a new political community, from scratch. We asserted that, in democratic societies, further crucial democratic advances could be carried out through a critical engagement with the existing institutions.

The problem with modern democratic societies, in our view, was that their constitutive principles of 'liberty and equality for all' were not put into practice. The task of the left was not to discard them but to fight for their effective implementation. The 'radical and plural democracy' that we advocated can therefore be conceived as a radicalization of the existing democratic institutions, with the result that the principles of liberty and equality become effective in an increasing number of social relations. This did not require a radical break of the revolutionary type, implying a total refoundation. Instead, it could be achieved in a hegemonic way, through an immanent critique that mobilizes the symbolic resources of the democratic tradition.

I consider that it is also in the mode of an immanent critique that a left populist strategy can intervene to challenge post-democracy and restore the centrality of the democratic values of equality and popular sovereignty. Such a mode of intervention is possible because, despite their relegation by neoliberalism, democratic values still play a significant role in the political imaginary of our societies. Furthermore, their critical meaning can be reactivated to subvert the hegemonic order and create a different one. This is corroborated by the fact that many resistances against the post-democratic condition are being expressed in the name of equality and popular sovereignty.

While there is no doubt that the current social and political regression has been brought about by neoliberal policies, it is notable that most of those protests do not take the form of a direct rejection of financial capitalism and of neoliberalism but of an indictment of the establishment elites seen as having imposed, without popular consultation, policies that privilege their interests.

Therefore it is through the language of democracy that many citizens can articulate their protests. It is no doubt significant that the main targets of the 'movement of the squares' were the shortcomings of the political system and of the democratic institutions and that they did not call for 'socialism' but for a 'real democracy'. Remember the motto of the Indignados in Spain: 'We have a vote but we do not have a voice.'

To inscribe the left populist strategy in the democratic tradition is, in my view, the decisive move because this establishes a connection with the political values that are central to popular aspirations. The fact that so many resistances against various forms of oppression are expressed as democratic demands testifies to the crucial role played by the signifier 'democracy' in the political imaginary. Of course, this signifier is often abused, but it has not lost its radical potential. When used critically, emphasizing its egalitarian dimension, it constitutes a powerful weapon in the hegemonic struggle to create a new common sense. Indeed, Gramsci suggested such a path when he asserted that it was 'not a question of introducing from scratch a scientific form of thought into everyone's individual life, but of renovating and making "critical" an already existing activity'.[1]

To apprehend the role of the democratic discourse in the constitution of political subjectivity, it is necessary to understand that political identities are not a direct expression of objective positions in the social order. This attests to the importance of an anti-essentialist approach in the field of politics. As asserted in *Hegemony and Socialist*

1   Antonio Gramsci, *Prison Notebooks* (London: Lawrence & Wishart, 1971), p. 330.

Strategy, there is nothing natural or inevitable in the struggles against relations of power, nor in the form that they will take.

The struggle against forms of subordination cannot be the direct result of the situation of subordination itself. For relations of subordination to be transformed into sites of an antagonism, one needs the presence of a discursive 'exterior' from which the discourse of subordination can be interrupted. This is precisely what the democratic discourse has made possible. It is thanks to the democratic discourse, which provides the main political vocabulary in Western societies, that relations of subordination can be put into question.

When did the principles of liberty and equality become the matrix of a democratic imaginary? The decisive mutation in the political imaginary of Western societies took place at the time of what Tocqueville called the 'democratic revolution'. As Claude Lefort has shown, its defining moment was the French Revolution with its novel affirmation of the absolute power of the people. This initiated a new symbolic mode of social institutions that broke with the theologico-political matrix and, with the *Declaration of the Rights of Man*, provided a vocabulary to question the different forms of inequality as illegitimate.[2] Tocqueville perceived the subversive character of what he called the 'passion for equality' when he wrote:

> It is impossible to believe that equality will not finally penetrate as much into the political world as into other domains. It is not possible to conceive of men as

2 Claude Lefort, *Democracy and Political Theory*, trans. David Macey (Cambridge, UK: Polity Press, 1988), chapter 1.

eternally unequal among themselves on one point, and
equal on others; at a certain moment, they will come to
be equal on all points.[3]

To be sure, as an aristocrat, Tocqueville did not celebrate
the coming of this new era, but he was resigned to its
inevitability. And what he predicted came true. From the
critique of political inequality, this 'passion for equality'
led, through the different socialist discourses and the
struggles that they informed, to the questioning of
economic inequality, thereby opening a new chapter of
the democratic revolution. With the development of the
'new social movements', a further chapter was opened,
the chapter in which we are now living, characterized by
the questioning of many other forms of inequality.

It is remarkable that, after more than 200 years, the
power of the democratic imaginary remains in force,
encouraging the pursuit of equality and liberty in a multiplicity of new domains. This should not make us believe,
however, that we are witnessing a linear and ineluctable
evolution towards an equal society, as the crimes perpe-
trated by the West during the last centuries clearly show.
Besides, as I have already indicated, liberty and equality
can never be perfectly reconciled and they are always in
tension.

More importantly, they only exist inscribed in different
hegemonic formations, under specific interpretations,
where their meaning can be contested. A hegemonic
formation is a configuration of social practices of different
natures: economic, cultural, political, and juridical, whose

3 Alexis de Tocqueville, *De la démocratie en Amérique*, vol. 1
(Paris: Flammarion, 1981), p. 115.

articulation is secured around some key symbolic signifi-
ers which shape the 'common sense' and provide the
normative framework of a given society. The objective of
the hegemonic struggle consists in disarticulating the sedimented practices of an existing formation and, through
the transformation of these practices and the instauration
of new ones, establishing the nodal points of a new hegemonic social formation. This process comports as a necessary step with the rearticulation of the hegemonic signifi-
ers and their mode of institutionalization. Clearly
articulating democracy with equal rights, social appropri-
ation of the means of production and popular sovereignty
will command a very different politics and inform different socioeconomic practices than when democracy was
articulated with the free market, private property and
unfettered individualism. We have seen how in the hegemonic transition to neoliberalism Margaret Thatcher
managed, thanks to her capacity to disentangle the social-
democratic articulation of liberty and equality, to promote
a new understanding of those values that made possible
the implementation of her neoliberal project.

To grasp what is at stake in the transition from one
hegemonic formation to another, it is necessary to make
a methodological distinction between two levels of analysis: the ethico-political principles of the liberal-democratic *politeia* and their different hegemonic forms of
inscription. Such distinction is crucial for democratic
politics because, by revealing the variety of hegemonic
formations compatible with a liberal-democratic form of
society, it helps us to visualize the difference between a
hegemonic transformation and a revolutionary rupture.

A liberal-democratic society supposes the existence of
an institutional order informed by the ethico-political

principles that constitute its principles of legitimacy. But this allows for a multiplicity of ways in which those principles are articulated and institutionalized in specific hegemonic formations. What is at stake in a hegemonic transformation is the constitution of a new historical bloc based on a different articulation between the constitutive political principles of the liberal-democratic regime and the socioeconomic practices in which they are institutionalized. In the case of a transition from one hegemonic order to another, those political principles remain in force, but they are interpreted and institutionalized in a different way. This is not the case with a 'revolution' understood as a total rupture with a political regime and the adoption of new principles of legitimacy.

The strategy of left populism seeks the establishment of a new hegemonic order within the constitutional liberal-democratic framework and it does not aim at a radical break with pluralist liberal democracy and the foundation of a totally new political order. Its objective is the construction of a collective will, a 'people' apt to bring about a new hegemonic formation that will reestablish the articulation between liberalism and democracy that has been disavowed by neoliberalism, putting democratic values in the leading role. The process of recovering and radicalizing democratic institutions will no doubt include moments of rupture and a confrontation with the dominant economic interests, but it does not require relinquishing the liberal-democratic principles of legitimacy.

Such a hegemonic strategy engages with the existing political institutions in view of transforming them through democratic procedures and it rejects the false dilemma between reform and revolution. It is therefore clearly different both from the revolutionary strategy of the 'extreme left' and from the sterile reformism of the social liberals who only seek a mere alternation in government. It could be called 'radical reformism' or, following Jean Jaures, 'revolutionary reformism' to indicate the subversive dimension of the reforms and the fact that what they pursue, although it is through democratic means, is a profound transformation of the structure of the socioeconomic power relations.

Within the spectrum of what is usually understood as 'the left', one could therefore differentiate three kinds of politics. The first is a 'pure reformism' that accepts both the principles of legitimacy of liberal democracy and the existing neoliberal hegemonic social formation. Second is the 'radical reformism' that accepts the principles of legitimacy but attempts to implement a different hegemonic formation. Finally, 'revolutionary politics' seeks a total rupture with the existing sociopolitical order. Under this third category we find not only the traditional Leninist politics but also other types, like those promoted by the anarchists or the advocates of 'insurrection' which call for a total rejection of the state and liberal-democratic institutions.

The nature and the role of the state constitute a central point of divergence between those three forms of 'left' politics. While the reformist view envisages the state as a neutral institution whose role is to reconcile the interests of the various social groups and the revolutionary one sees it as an oppressive institution that has to be abolished, the radical reformist perspective addresses the question of the state in a different way. Taking its bearings from Gramsci, it conceives the state as a crystallization of the relations of forces and as a terrain of struggle. It is not a homogeneous medium but an uneven set of branches and functions, only relatively integrated by the hegemonic practices that take place within it.

One of Gramsci's key contributions to hegemonic politics is his conception of the 'integral state', which he conceived as including both political society *and* civil society. This should not be understood as a 'statization' of civil society but an indication of the profoundly political character of civil society, presented as the terrain of the struggle for hegemony. In this view, next to the traditional apparatus of government, the state is also composed of a variety of apparatuses and public spaces where different forces contend for hegemony.

Envisaged as a surface for agonistic interventions, these public spaces can provide the terrain for important democratic advances. This is why a hegemonic strategy should engage with the diverse state apparatuses in order to transform them, so as to make the state a vehicle for the expression of the manifold of democratic demands. What is at stake is not the 'withering away' of the state and of the institutions through which pluralism is organized, but a profound transformation of those institutions to put them at the service of a process of radicalization of democracy. The objective is not the *seizure* of state power but, as Gramsci put it, one of '*becoming* state'.

How to understand 'radical' politics according to this perspective? In a certain sense, both the revolutionary type of politics and the hegemonic one can be called 'radical' as they imply a form of rupture with the existing hegemonic order. However, this rupture is not of the same nature and it is inappropriate to put them in the same category labelled 'extreme left', as is often the case.

Contrary to what is often claimed, the left populist strategy is not an avatar of the 'extreme left' but a different way of envisaging the rupture with neoliberalism through the recovery and radicalization of democracy. The current move by the defenders of the status quo to label all of the critiques of the neoliberal order 'extreme left', and to present them as a danger to democracy, is a disingenuous attempt to impede any kind of challenge to the existing hegemonic order. As if the choice was limited to accepting the current neoliberal hegemonic formation as the only legitimate form of liberal democracy or rejecting liberal democracy altogether.

It is interesting to note that we find the same dilemma in those on the left who affirm that the radicalization of democracy requires relinquishing liberal democracy. In several cases, this false dilemma proceeds from the widespread confusion between the political institutions of liberal democracy and the capitalist mode of production. While it is true that such an articulation is the one that we have so far encountered historically, it is a contingent one.

Despite the claim of many liberal theorists that political liberalism necessarily entails economic liberalism and that a democratic society requires a capitalist economy, it is clear that there is no necessary relationship between capitalism and liberal democracy. It is unfortunate that Marxism has contributed to this confusion by presenting liberal democracy as the superstructure of capitalism. It is really regrettable that this economistic approach is still accepted in several sectors of the left that call for the destruction of the liberal state. It is within the framework of the constitutive principles of the liberal state – the division of power, universal suffrage, multi-party systems and civil rights – that it will be possible to advance the full range of present-day democratic demands. To struggle against post-democracy does not consist in discarding those principles but in defending and radicalizing them.

This does not mean accepting the capitalist order as the only possible one and, although it remains within the liberal-democratic political framework, the politics of radical reformism that I advocate is not thereby prevented in challenging the capitalist relations of production. This is why it is important to distinguish between political liberalism and economic liberalism.

The process of radicalizing democracy necessarily includes an anti-capitalist dimension as many of the forms of subordination that will need to be challenged are the consequences of capitalist relations of production. However, there is no reason to assume that the working class has an *a priori* privileged role in the anti-capitalist struggle. Indeed, there are no *a priori* privileged places in the anti-capitalist struggle. There are many points of antagonism between capitalism and various sectors of the population, and this means that, when this struggle is envisaged as an extension of the democratic principles, there will be a variety of anti-capitalist struggles. In some cases they might not even be perceived as being 'anti-capitalist' by people involved in them and many will be conducted in the name of equality and conceived as struggles for democracy.

People do not fight against 'capitalism' as an abstract entity because they believe in a 'law of history' leading to socialism. It is always on the basis of concrete situations that they are moved to act. If they struggle for equality it is because their resistances to various forms of domination are informed by democratic values and it is around those values, addressing their actual aspirations and subjectivities, and not in the name of anti-capitalism, that people can be mobilized. Even Marxists like David Harvey seem to agree with this perspective; Harvey writes: 'It is the profoundly anti-democratic nature of neoliberalism backed by the authoritarianism of the neo-conservatives that should surely be the main focus of social struggle.'[4]

The fundamental mistake of the 'extreme left' has always been to ignore this. They do not engage with how people are in reality, but with how they should be according to their theories. As a result, they see their role as making them realise the 'truth' about their situation. Instead of designating the adversaries in ways that people can identify, they use abstract categories like 'capitalism', thereby failing to mobilize the affective dimension necessary to motivate people to act politically. They are in fact insensitive to people's effective demands. Their anti-capitalist rhetoric does not find any echo in the groups whose interests they pretend to represent. This is why they always remain in marginal positions.

The objective of a left populist strategy is the creation of a popular majority to come to power and establish a progressive hegemony. There is no blueprint for how this will take place or a final destination. The chain of equivalence through which the 'people' is going to be constituted will depend on the historical circumstances. Its dynamics cannot be determined in isolation from all contextual reference.

The same is true for the shape of the new hegemony that this strategy seeks to bring about. What is in

4   David Harvey, *A Brief History of Neoliberalism* (New York: Oxford University Press, 2005).

question is not the establishment of a 'populist regime' with a pre-defined programme but the creation of a hegemonic formation that will foster the recovery and deepening of democracy. This hegemony will take different names according to the specific trajectories involved. It could be envisaged as 'democratic socialism', 'eco-socialism', 'associative democracy' or 'participatory democracy'; everything depends on the contexts and national traditions.

What is important, whatever the name, is the recognition that 'democracy' is the hegemonic signifier around which the diverse struggles are articulated and that political liberalism is not discarded. An appropriate term could be 'liberal socialism' by which Norberto Bobbio refers to a social formation that combines liberal-democratic institutions and an economic framework with several socialist characteristics.

Understanding socialism as the democratization of the state and of the economy, Bobbio asserts in several works where he examines the articulation between socialism and liberal democracy that a democratic socialism needs to be a liberal one.[5] Visualizing the objective of socialism as the deepening of liberal democratic values, he is adamant that the realization of its goals does not require a break with constitutional government and the rule of law. He forcefully defends the idea that the socialist goals could be realized within the framework of liberal democracy, insisting that they could only be realized within such a framework.

5 See, for instance, Norberto Bobbio, *The Future of Democracy: A Defence of the Rules of the Game*, trans. Roger Griffin (London: Polity Press, 1987) and *Which Socialism?: Marxism, Socialism and Democracy*, trans. Roger Griffin (London: Polity Press, 1987).

Envisaged in such a way, the project of the radicalization of democracy shares some characteristics with social democracy before its conversion to social liberalism, but it is not a simple return to the postwar model of compromise between capital and labour. Such a comparison would not work anymore. Besides the necessity of taking account of the new democratic demands, the defence of the environment is clearly one of the main reasons why a return to the postwar model is not possible. By promoting consumer demand and economic growth, Keynesian solutions are the motors of environmental destruction. As I will argue in the next chapter, to face the challenge of the ecological crisis a radical democratic project needs to articulate the ecological and social questions. It is necessary to imagine a new synthesis between key aspects of the democratic and socialist traditions around a new model of development.

As I indicated at the beginning of this chapter, there are many ways to conceive of radical democracy and the differences and disagreements are worth considering. The principal disagreement between my definition and several others concerns the question of representative democracy, which is often declared to be an oxymoron by several radical democratic theorists. Some of them claim, for instance, that the protest movements that we have been witnessing in recent years signal the demise of the representative model and represent a call for a nonrepresentative democracy, a 'democracy *in actu*'. In *Agonistics* I criticized this view and argued that we were not facing a crisis of representative democracy 'per se' but a crisis of its current post-democratic incarnation.[6]

6 Chantal Mouffe, *Agonistics: Thinking the World Politically* (London and New York: Verso, 2013), chapter 6.

This crisis is due to the absence of an agonistic confrontation and the solution cannot reside in the establishment of a 'non-representative' democracy. Taking issue with the idea that extra-parliamentary struggles were the only vehicle for making democratic advances, I asserted that, instead of the strategy of desertion and exodus advocated by Michael Hardt and Antonio Negri, what was needed was a strategy of 'engagement' with the state and with representative institutions, with the aim of profoundly transforming them.

It is interesting to note that in *Assembly*, Hardt and Negri have significantly changed their position with respect to the strategy of exodus. They now declare that the Multitude should not follow the path of exodus and withdrawal and that it cannot avoid the need to take power, but they insist on the need 'to take power differently'.[7] What this means is not very clear and in any case they do not seem to have abandoned their idea that the Multitude could auto-organize itself. If they now recognize the role of leadership, they contend that it must be limited to making tactical decisions, while the strategic ones should be reserved for the Multitude. As they put it:

'Leadership' must be constantly subordinated to the multitude, deployed and dismissed as occasion dictates. If leaders are still necessary and possible in this context, it is only because they serve the productive multitude. This is not an elimination of leadership, then, but an inversion of the political relationship that constitutes it,

7   Michael Hardt and Antonio Negri, *Assembly* (New York: Oxford University Press, 2017), p. 288.

a reversal of the polarity that links horizontal movements and vertical leadership.[8]

They claim, thanks to this reversal, to be able to avoid the
problem facing all types of populism, both from the left
and from the right, which are 'characterized by a central
paradox: constant lip service to the power of the people
but ultimate control and decision-making by a small
clique of politicians'.[9]

Central to the perspective of Hardt and Negri is the
notion of 'the common', which, defined in contrast to
property both private and public, constitutes the linchpin
of their approach. In this respect *Assembly* follows their
previous analyses in *Commonwealth*, where they argue
that bio-political production creates the condition for a
democracy of the multitude because it produces the forms
of economic and political subjectivities that are an expression of 'the common'. As labour is increasingly responsible for generating cooperation without the need for the
intervention of capital, bio-political production brings
with it new democratic capacities. According to them a
society built on the principle of 'the common' is therefore
already evolving through the processes of informatization
and the development of cognitive capitalism.

Independently of the value of their analysis of the
productive process, which has been criticized from many
quarters, what I find problematic in their celebration of
'the common' is the idea that it might provide the main
principle of organization of society. The central problem
with this celebration of 'the common', which is found,

8   Ibid., p. xv.
9   Ibid., p. 23.

albeit in different forms, in the work of many other theorists is that, by postulating a conception of multiplicity that is free from negativity and antagonism, it does not make room for the recognition of the necessarily hegemonic nature of the social order. In the case of Hardt and Negri, their refusal of representation and sovereignty proceeds from an immanentist ontology that is clearly in contradiction with the one that informs my conception of radical democracy.

One can also find a critique of representation in another proposal to radicalize democracy. In this case the ancient practice of selection by lot, sortition, is presented by a variety of theorists as providing the remedy to the crisis of representation currently affecting our democratic societies. Such proponents claim that representative democracy has been invented to exclude the people from power and that the only way to establish a real democratic order is to abandon the electoral model and replace it with a lottery.[10]

This view is flawed because it reduces representation to elections and does not acknowledge the role of representation in a pluralist democracy. Society is divided and crisscrossed by power relations and antagonisms, and representative institutions play a crucial role in allowing for the institutionalization of this conflictual dimension. For example, in a pluralist democracy, political parties provide discursive frameworks that allow people to make sense of the social world in which they are inscribed and to perceive its fault lines.

If we accept that the consciousness of the social agent is not the direct expression of their 'objective' position and

10   See, for instance, David Van Reybrouck, *Against Elections: The Case for Democracy*, trans. Liz Waters (London: Vintage, 2016).

that it is always discursively constructed, it is clear that political subjectivities will be shaped by competing political discourses and that parties are essential in their elaboration. They provide symbolic markers allowing people to situate themselves in the social world and to give meaning to their lived experiences. In recent years, however, these symbolic spaces have increasingly been occupied by other discourses of various natures, and this has had very negative consequences for a democratic society. Due to the post-political turn, parties have lost their power to play a symbolic role, but this should not lead us to the conclusion that democracy could do without them. As I have repeatedly argued, a pluralist democratic society which does not envisage pluralism in a harmonious anti-political form and where the ever-present possibility of antagonism is acknowledged cannot exist without representation.

An effective pluralism supposes the presence of an agonistic confrontation between hegemonic projects. It is through representation that collective political subjects are created; they do not exist beforehand. Instead of trying to look for a solution to the crisis of democracy in a model like sortition, which does not recognize the collective nature of the political subject and envisages the exercise of democracy on the basis of individual viewpoints, it is urgent to restore the agonistic dynamics constitutive of a vibrant democracy. Far from being a procedure apt to enact a better democracy, selection by lot promotes a vision of politics as the terrain where individuals, unencumbered by constitutive social links, would defend their personal opinions.

The main problem with existing representative institutions is that they do not allow for the agonistic confrontation between different projects of society which is the very condition of a vibrant democracy. It is this lack of an agonistic confrontation, not the fact of representation, which deprives the citizens of a voice. The remedy does not lie in abolishing representation but in making our institutions more representative. This is indeed the objective of a left populist strategy.

4

The Construction of a People

When Ernesto Laclau and I wrote *Hegemony and Socialist Strategy*, the challenge for left-wing politics was to recognize the demands of the 'new movements' and the need to articulate them alongside more traditional workers' demands. Nowadays the recognition and legitimacy of these demands have significantly progressed and many of them have been integrated into the left agenda. In fact it could be argued that the situation today is the opposite of the one we criticized thirty years ago, and that it is 'working-class' demands that are now neglected.

Another difference between now and then is that neoliberalism is at the origin of many new antagonisms that, like those arising from the destruction of the welfare state, affect numerous sectors of the population. Some of these antagonisms are due to the phenomenon of what David Harvey calls 'accumulation by dispossession'. By that term Harvey refers to the centralization of wealth and power in the hands of a few through a series of key practices of neoliberalism like privatization and financialization. He underlines the novelty of the struggles to which those practices give rise:

Accumulation by dispossession entails a very different set of practices from accumulation through the expansion of wage labour in industry and agriculture. The latter, which dominated processes of capital accumulation in the 1950s and 1960s, gave rise to an oppositional culture (such as that embedded in trade unions and working-class political parties) that produced embedded liberalism. Dispossession, on the other hand, is fragmented and particular – a privatization here, an environmental degradation there, a financial crisis of indebtedness somewhere else.[1]

From another theoretical perspective, the emergence of new antagonisms is also underlined by theorists who point to the pervasive effects of bio-political neoliberal forms of governmentality in all domains of life.

There is no doubt that under neoliberalism, the field of conflict has significantly widened. In a sense, this provides an opportunity, since the number of people affected by the neoliberal policies is much higher than those who are usually considered traditional left voters. A project of radicalization of democracy could therefore appeal to constituencies which so far have not identified with the left and, thanks to an adequate hegemonic politics, more people than before could be recruited for a progressive alternative. Nonetheless, this also makes the articulation of democratic demands in a collective will more complex because we are now faced with a greater variety and heterogeneity of them.

The challenge for a left populist strategy consists in reasserting the importance of the 'social question', taking

1   David Harvey, *A Brief History of Neoliberalism* (New York: Oxford University Press, 2005), p. 178.

account of the increasing fragmentation and diversity of the 'workers' but also of the specificity of the various democratic demands. This requires the construction of 'a people' around a project which addresses the diverse forms of subordination around issues concerning exploitation, domination or discrimination. A special emphasis must also be given to a question that has gained particular relevance in the last thirty years and which is of a special urgency today: the future of the planet.

It is impossible to envisage a project of radicalization of democracy in which the 'ecological question' is not at the centre of the agenda. It is therefore essential to combine this with the social question. No doubt this will require profound changes in our way of life and multifarious resistances will have to be overcome. To abandon the productivist model and to implement the necessary ecological transition will require a truly Gramscian 'intellectual and moral reform'. This will certainly not be easy, but an ambitious and well-designed ecological project could offer an attractive vision of a future democratic society that might entice some sectors currently within the neoliberal hegemonic bloc.

It is often said that the main cleavage in our societies is between the 'losers' and the 'winners' of neoliberal globalization and that their interests cannot be reconciled. Such a fracture does exist and there is clearly an antagonism between the two camps, an antagonism that cannot be visualized simply as a confrontation between 99% versus 1%. Nevertheless I believe that among the sectors who benefit from the neoliberal model, some might become aware of the grave dangers that it conveys for the environment and could be won over for a project of society that will guarantee a human future for their offspring. Hopefully, launching a counter-hegemonic struggle against the neoliberal model in the name of democratic and ecological values might help to dislocate the historical bloc on which it relies, thereby expanding the range of a radical democratic collective will.

I am aware that among those who are in favour of radicalizing democracy, not everybody considers it necessary or even desirable to articulate the diverse struggles in a collective will. In fact, a frequent objection to a left populist strategy is that to bring together the democratic demands in the creation of a 'people' will produce a homogeneous subject, one that negates plurality. Any attempt to do so should be rejected because it will erase the specificity of the various struggles. Another objection, slightly different, is that 'the people' as conceived by populism is from the start envisaged as being homogeneous and that this perspective is incompatible with democratic pluralism.

Such objections stem from the failure (or the refusal?) to grasp that a left populist strategy is informed by an anti-essentialist approach according to which the 'people' is not an empirical referent but a discursive political construction. It does not exist previously to its performative articulation and cannot be apprehended through sociological categories. Those critiques reveal a lack of understanding of the operation through which a people is constructed. As a collective will created through a chain of equivalence, the people is not a homogeneous subject in which all the differences are somehow reduced to unity.

We are not faced, as is often claimed, with a 'mass' as understood by Gustave Le Bon, where all differentiation disappears to create a totally homogeneous group. Instead we find ourselves within a process of articulation in which an equivalence is established between a multiplicity of heterogeneous demands in a way which maintains the internal differentiation of the group. As Ernesto Laclau specifies, 'This means that each individual demand is constitutively split: on the one hand it is its own particularized self; on the other it points, through equivalential links, to the totality of the other demands.'[2]

As Laclau and I have repeatedly stressed, a relation of equivalence is not one in which all differences collapse into identity but in which differences are still active. If such differences were eliminated, that would not be equivalence but a simple identity. It is only to the extent that democratic differences are opposed to forces or discourses that negate all of them that these differences can be substituted for each other. This is precisely why the creation of a collective will through a chain of equivalence demands the designation of an adversary. Such a move is necessary to draw the political frontier separating the 'we' from the 'they', which is decisive in the construction of a 'people'.

I would like to emphasize that a 'chain of equivalence' is not a simple coalition of existing political subjects. Nor are we dealing with a situation in which an already constituted people confronts a preexisting adversary. The people and the political frontier that defines its adversary are constructed through political struggle, and they are always susceptible to rearticulation through counter-hegemonic interventions. The democratic demands that a left populist strategy seeks to articulate are heterogeneous

2 Ernesto Laclau, 'Populism: What's in a Name?', in *Populism and the Mirror of Democracy*, ed. Francisco Panizza (New York and London: Verso, 2005), p. 37.

and this is why they need to be articulated in a chain of equivalence.

This process of articulation is crucial because it is by their inscription in this chain that singular demands acquire their political signification. It is not so much where those demands come from that counts, but how they are articulated with other demands. As the example of right populism testifies, demands for democracy can be articulated in a xenophobic vocabulary and they do not automatically have a progressive character. It is only by entering in equivalence with other democratic demands, like those of the immigrants or the feminists, that they acquire a radical democratic dimension. This is of course also true for the demands proceeding from women, immigrants or other groups discriminated against.

We should never take for granted that there are struggles that are inherently emancipatory and cannot be oriented towards opposite ends. The current development of forms of ecology with clear anti-democratic characteristics should be seen as a warning that the refusal of the neoliberal model is not a guarantee of a democratic advance. With ecology, as in other domains, the question of articulation is decisive and this is why it is essential to establish a link between ecological and social questions around the identification with a project of radicalization of democracy.

How to envisage an identification with radical democracy in a way congruent with my earlier claim that the chain of equivalence does not produce a homogeneous subject? To adequately address that question requires conceiving of the social agent as constructed within specific discourses corresponding to the multiplicity of social relations in which it is inscribed. Among those social relations, there is one which corresponds to the insertion of the social agent in a political community – that is, to its position as a 'citizen'.

It is *qua* citizen that a social agent intervenes at the level of the political community. While being a central category in a pluralist liberal democracy, citizenship can be understood in a variety of ways that command very different conceptions of politics. Liberalism envisages citizenship as a mere legal status and sees the citizen as an individual bearer of rights, free from any identification with a 'we'. In the democratic tradition, however, citizenship is conceived of as active involvement in the political community, as acting as part of 'we', in accordance with a certain conception of the general interest. This is why the fostering of a radical democratic conception of citizenship is a key in the fight against post-democracy.

To develop such a conception, we might find a source of inspiration in the civic republican tradition with its emphasis on active participation in the political community. When reformulated in a way that makes room for pluralism, civic republicanism in the 'plebeian' version inspired by Machiavelli can contribute to reasserting the importance of collective action and the value of the public realm that have been constantly under attack during the years of neoliberal hegemony.

The liberal and the democratic views have always been at loggerheads but, during the period of the Keynesian welfare state, liberal individualism was kept in check by social-democratic practices. On the whole, social-democratic common sense prevailed, until it was undermined by the neoliberal offensive. We have seen how under Thatcherism the citizen was replaced by the 'taxpayer', the political idea of liberty articulated with the economic idea of the free market and democracy reduced to electoral procedures. A crucial battle in the counter-hegemonic struggle against neoliberal hegemony consists in re-signifying the 'public' as the domain where citizens can have a voice and exercise their rights, displacing the individualistic and currently dominant conception of the citizen as a 'consumer' that is the linchpin of the post-democratic vision.

In *The Return of the Political*,[3] I proposed a conception of citizenship as a 'grammar of conduct' governed by the ethico-political principles of the liberal democratic *politeia*: liberty and equality for all. Since these principles can be interpreted in different manners, there are various ways in which one can identify and act as a democratic citizen. A social-democratic conception of citizenship, for instance, privileges the struggle for social and economic rights, while a radical democratic interpretation highlights the numerous other social relations where relations of domination exist and need to be challenged for the principles of liberty and equality to apply. Conceived as providing the common identification of persons involved in diverse democratic struggles, a radical democratic conception of citizenship could constitute the locus of construction of a 'people' through a chain of equivalence. Identifying as citizens whose political objective is the radicalization of democracy is what would unite social agents, who might be engaged in many different enterprises but whose 'grammar of conduct', when acting *qua* citizens, is governed by the extension of the

3 Chantal Mouffe, *The Return of the Political* (New York and London: Verso, 1993), chapter 4.

ethico-political principles of liberty and equality to a wide range of social relations.

Next to issues that concern the social agent as inscribed in specific social relations – where intersectional struggles for liberty and equality take place – there are other issues that necessitate acting together in view of transforming the state, which is essential for the formulation of a radical democratic project. Many of the egalitarian objectives that it pursues, for instance in the domain of education, can only be reached thanks to state intervention. This intervention should not be envisaged in a bureaucratic and authoritarian way, and the role of the state should be to provide the conditions for citizens to take charge of the public services and organize them democratically.

Conceiving citizenship as a political 'grammar of conduct' shows that it is possible to be part of a 'people' identified with a radical democratic project, while being at the same time inscribed in a plurality of other social relations with their specific 'subjectivities'. To act *qua* citizen at the political level to radicalize democracy does not mean discarding other forms of identification and is perfectly compatible with being involved in democratic struggles of a more punctual nature. Indeed, a radical democratic citizenship encourages such a plurality of engagements. This is why a left populist strategy requires the articulation between interventions at the 'vertical' and the 'horizontal' level, inside representative institutions as well as in various associations and social movements. It also aims to create a synergy between the manifold practices where various forms of domination are challenged and those that experiment with new egalitarian forms of life.

For instance, those who are involved *qua* citizens in the political project of Podemos or La France Insoumise will intervene in diverse representative institutions, while also being engaged in a variety of democratic practices and struggles focusing on more specific issues. To partake in a 'we' of radical democratic citizens does not preclude participation in a variety of other 'we's'.

There is a point, though, that should be clarified here. The extension of the field of exercise of citizenship that I am proposing does not imply that all democratic decisions are to be made by social agents in their quality of citizens. It is important to distinguish between issues that concern them *qua* members of a political community and those which have to do with other social relations and concern particular communities. Otherwise one might end up with a totalizing view that negates the pluralism which is vital for a radical democratic conception that respects the value of liberty.

The radical democratic conception of citizenship that I am proposing is closely linked with the radical reformist politics of engagement with the institutions that I advocated earlier. It sees the state as an important scene in democratic politics because it constitutes the space where citizens can make decisions about the organization of the political community. It is indeed where popular sovereignty can be exercised. This supposes, however, that the conditions exist for an agonistic confrontation and this is why it is indispensable to break with the neoliberal post-political consensus.

Contrary to what liberals pretend, the state is not a neutral terrain. It is always hegemonically structured and it constitutes a significant site for the counter-hegemonic struggle. However, it is not the only site of intervention, and opposition between party and movements, or between parliamentary and extra-parliamentary struggles should be rejected. According to an agonistic model of democracy, there exists a multiplicity of agonistic public spaces where one should intervene to radicalize democracy. The traditional political space of parliament is not the only one where political decisions are made and, while representative institutions should retain, or regain, a decisive role, new forms of democratic participation are necessary to radicalize democracy.

I argued in the previous chapter against a purely horizontalist conception of radical democracy, but that does not mean that I am in favour of representative democracy in its present form. The project of radicalization of democracy that I am proposing envisages a combination of different forms of democratic participation, depending on the spaces and social relations where liberty and equality should be implemented. One could imagine an articulation of various forms of representation and modes of choosing representatives. Direct forms of democracy might be suitable in some cases and a variety of participative ones in others. Although I am critical of direct democracy or sortition, when imagined as the exclusive mode of political decision making, I would have no problem allowing them a place in specific cases, in conjunction with representative institutions. There are indeed many ways to enhance representative democracy and make it more accountable. With respect to the fashionable idea of 'the common', while I find it inappropriate as a general principle of organization of society, I think that in several domains practices of 'commoning' can play an important role in fighting against processes of privatization of goods that, like water, should be recognized as part of 'the commons'. As long as the political model that is suggested acknowledges the fact that society is divided and that every order is hegemonically structured, many possible configurations of democratic procedures are possible.

To the previous consideration about citizenship, I would like to add that the hegemonic operation of constructing a people requires an articulating principle to connect in a chain of equivalence the manifold democratic demands constituting the collective will. This articulating principle will vary according to the different conjunctures and it can be provided either by a specific democratic demand that becomes the symbol of the common struggle for the radicalization of democracy, or by the figure of a leader.

The role of the leader in the populist strategy has always been a subject of criticism and it is the reason why those movements are often accused of being authoritarian. Many people find charismatic leadership very dangerous and no doubt it can have negative effects. But independently of the fact that it is very difficult to find examples of important political movements without prominent leaders, there is no reason to equate strong leadership with authoritarianism. Everything depends on the kind of relation that is established between the leader and the people. In the case of right-wing populism, it is a very authoritarian relation where everything comes from the top without real grassroots participation.

But the leader can be conceived of as a *primus inter pares* and it is perfectly possible to establish a different type of relation, less vertical between the leader and the people. Moreover, as I will argue in a moment, a collective will cannot be constructed without some form of crystallization of common affects, and affective bonds with a charismatic leader can play an important role in this process.

Another frequent criticism addressed to the left populist strategy is the role it attributes to the national dimension. This raises a series of questions, like the membership of the European Union, that go beyond the scope of this book, which is not concerned with specific policies but only with the kind of strategy apt, in the current conjuncture, to bring about a collective will aiming at a hegemonic transformation. Once such a transformation has taken place, the conditions will exist for an agonistic debate about the policies more suitable for radicalizing democracy and the answers should not be determined in advance.

What I want to underline is that the hegemonic struggle to recover democracy needs to start at the level of the nation state that, despite having lost many of its prerogatives, is still one of the crucial spaces for the exercise of democracy and popular sovereignty. It is at the national level that the question of radicalizing democracy must first be posed. This is where a collective will to resist the post-democratic effects of neoliberal globalization should be constructed. It is only when this collective will has been consolidated that collaboration with similar movements in other countries can be productive. It is clear that the struggle against neoliberalism cannot be won at the national level alone and it is necessary to establish an alliance at the European level. But a left populist strategy cannot ignore the strong libidinal investment at work in national – or regional – forms of identification and it would be very risky to abandon this terrain to right-wing populism. This does not mean following its example in promoting closed and defensive forms of nationalism, but instead offering another outlet for those affects, mobilizing them around a patriotic identification with the best and more egalitarian aspects of the national tradition.

Now we need to consider a question that I take to be crucial for envisaging the construction of a 'people': the decisive role played by affects in the constitution of political identities. The lack of understanding of the affective dimension in the processes of identification is, in my view, one of the main reasons for which the left, locked in a rationalist framework, is unable to grasp the dynamics of politics. This rationalism is no doubt at the origin of the stubborn refusal of so many left theorists to accept the teachings of psychoanalysis.

This is a serious flaw because Freud's critique of the idea of the unified character of the subject and his claim that the human mind is necessarily subject to division between two systems, of which one is not and cannot be conscious, are of vital importance for politics. Freud shows that, far from being organized around the transparency of an ego, personality is structured on a number of levels that lie outside of the consciousness and rationality of the agents. He therefore obliges us to abandon one of the key tenets of rationalist philosophy – the category of the subject as a rational, transparent entity able to confer a homogeneous meaning on the totality of her conduct – and to accept that 'individuals' are mere referential identities, resulting from the articulation between localized subject positions. The claim of psychoanalysis that there are no essential identities but only forms of identification is at the centre of the anti-essentialist approach that stipulates that the history of the subject is the history of her identifications and that there is no concealed identity to be rescued beyond the latter.

Taking its bearings from Freud, this approach acknowledges that an important dimension of politics is the construction of political identities and that this always entails an affective dimension. In *Group Psychology and the Analysis of the Ego*, Freud highlighted the decisive role played by affective libidinal bonds in processes of collective identification: 'A group is clearly held together by a power of some kind: and to what power could this feat be better ascribed than to Eros, which holds together everything in the world.'[4]

To recognize the role of this libidinal energy and the fact that it is malleable and can be oriented in multiple directions, producing different affects, is essential for understanding the work of the hegemonic operation. The fostering of a collective will aiming at the radicalization of democracy requires mobilizing affective energy through inscription in discursive practices that beget identification with a democratic egalitarian vision. Let me remind you that by 'discursive practice', I am not referring to a practice concerned exclusively with speech or writing but to signifying practices in which signification and action, linguistic and affective components cannot be separated. It is through their insertion in discursive/affective signifying practices, involving words, affects and actions that social agents acquire forms of subjectivity.

To envisage those discursive/affective inscriptions, we can find important insights in Spinoza, whose notion of '*conatus*' has affinities with Freud's 'libido'. Like Freud, Spinoza believes that it is desire that moves human beings to act and he notes that what makes them act in one direction rather than in another are the affects. In a reflection on the affects in his *Ethics,* Spinoza makes a distinction between affection (*affectio*) and affect

4 Sigmund Freud, *Group Psychology and the Analysis of the Ego*, in *The Standard Edition of the Complete Psychological Works of Sigmund Freud*, vol. XVIII (London: Vintage, 2001), p. 92.

(*affectus*).[5] An 'affection' is a state of a body insofar as it is subject to the action of another body. When affected by something exterior, the *conatus* (the general striving to persevere in our being) will experience affects that will move it to desire something and to act accordingly.

I suggest deploying this dynamic of *affectio/affectus* to examine the process of formation of political identities, seeing 'affections' as the practices where the discursive and the affective are articulated, producing specific forms of identification. Envisaged as crystallization of affects, those identifications are crucial for politics because they provide the motor of political action.

The hegemonic approach has been criticized by some theorists of the 'affective turn', who claim that this approach only takes account of the discursive dimension. Refuting this criticism, Yannis Stavrakakis has shown how it is those who advocate a 'post-hegemonic' approach who are in the wrong because, by separating the discursive from the affective, they miss their constitutive inter-implication.[6] On the contrary, the discursive theory of hegemony acknowledges such inter-implications when it asserts that 'something belonging to the order of affect has a primary role in discursively constructing the social.'[7]

---

5 Benedictus de Spinoza, *Ethics*, trans. Edwin Curley (New York: Penguin, 1994), part 3.

6 Yannis Stavrakakis, 'Hegemony or Post-hegemony? Discourse, Representation and the Revenge(s) of the Real', in *Radical Democracy and Collective Movements Today: The Biopolitics of the Multitude Versus the Hegemony of the People*, ed. Alexandros Kioupkiolis and Giorgos Katsambekis (New York: Ashgate, 2014).

7 Ernesto Laclau, 'Glimpsing the Future: A Reply', in *Laclau: A Critical Reader*, ed. Simon Critchley and Oliver Marchart (New York: Routledge, 2004), p. 326.

Some of the promoters of the 'affective turn' present their view of affect as based on the thought of Spinoza, but there are good reasons to question such genealogy. I find much more convincing the interpretation of Frédéric Lordon who, in his reading of the role of affects in Spinoza, underlines how for him politics is an *ars effectandi*, which deals with the production of ideas with the power to affect (*idées affectantes*).[8] Questioning the privilege accorded by Marxism to the material determinations and the problematic antinomy that it establishes between matter and ideas, Lordon shows how Spinoza allows us to transcend it through the notion of 'affection' which results as much from ideas as from material determinations. It is when the junction between ideas and affects takes place that ideas acquire power.

When envisaging discursive/affective practices, we can also take inspiration from Wittgenstein, who taught us that it is by their inscription in 'language games' (what we call discursive practices) that social agents form specific beliefs and desires and acquire their subjectivity. Following his approach, we can envisage allegiance to democracy, not as based on rationality but as participation in specific forms of life. As Richard Rorty has often pointed out, a Wittgensteinian perspective makes us realize that allegiance to democracy and the belief in the value of its institutions does not depend on giving democracy an intellectual foundation.

Allegiance to democratic values is a question of identification. It is created not through rational argumentation but through an ensemble of language

8 Frédéric Lordon, *Les Affects de la politique* (Paris: Seuil, 2016), p. 57.

games that construct democratic forms of individuality. Wittgenstein clearly acknowledges the affective dimension of different modes of allegiance when he likens religious belief to 'a passionate commitment to a system of reference'.[9] Bringing together Spinoza, Freud and Wittgenstein, we can see inscription in discursive practices as providing the affections that for Spinoza bring about the affects that spur desire and lead to specific action. It is recognized in this way that affects and desire play a crucial role in the constitution of collective forms of identification.

Recognizing the crucial role played by affects in politics and how they can be mobilized is decisive for designing a successful left populist strategy. Such a strategy should follow Gramsci's lead when he calls for 'an organic cohesion in which feeling-passion becomes understanding'. Working with notions from the 'common sense', it should address people in a manner able to reach their affects. It has to be congruent with the values and the identities of those that it seeks to interpellate and must connect with the aspects of popular experience. To resonate with the problems people encounter in their daily lives, it needs to start from where they are and how they feel, offering them a vision of the future that gives them hope, instead of remaining in the register of denunciation.

A left populist strategy aims at the crystallization of a collective will sustained by common affects aspiring for a more democratic order. This requires the creation of a different regime of desires and affects through inscription

9 Ludwig Wittgenstein, *Culture and Value*, trans. Peter Winch (Chicago: University of Chicago Press, 1984), p. 64.

in discursive/affective practices that will bring about new forms of identification. Those discursive/affective practices are of various natures, but the cultural and artistic fields constitute a very important terrain for the constitution of different forms of subjectivity.

Here again, Gramsci is an indispensable guide because he has shown the centrality of the cultural domain in the formation and diffusion of the 'common sense' that commands a specific definition of reality. Seeing 'common sense' as the result of a discursive articulation permits us to understand how it can be transformed thanks to counter-hegemonic interventions. Highlighting the decisive role of artistic and cultural practices in the hegemonic struggle, I argued in *Agonistics* that if artistic practices can play a decisive role in the construction of new forms of subjectivity, it is because, in using resources that induce emotional responses, they are able to reach human beings at the affective level.[10] This is indeed where lies art's great power, in its capacity to make us see things in a different way, to make us perceive new possibilities.

Artistic and cultural practices have for that reason an important role to play in a left populist strategy. To maintain its hegemony, the neoliberal system needs to constantly mobilize people's desires and shape their identities. The construction of a 'people' apt to build a different hegemony requires cultivating a multiplicity of discursive/affective practices that would erode the common affects that sustain the neoliberal hegemony and create the conditions for a radicalization of democracy. It is essential for a left

10 Chantal Mouffe, *Agonistics: Thinking the World Politically* (London and New York: Verso, 2013), chapter 5.

populist strategy to acknowledge the importance of fostering common affects because, as Spinoza was keen to stress, an affect can only be displaced by an opposed affect, stronger than the one to be repressed.

Conclusion

Examining the current conjuncture in Western Europe, I have argued that we are living through a 'populist moment'. This is the expression of resistances against the post-democratic condition brought about by thirty years of neoliberal hegemony. This hegemony has now entered into crisis and this is creating the opportunity for the establishment of a new hegemonic formation. This new hegemonic formation could be either more authoritarian or more democratic, depending on how those resistances are going to be articulated and the type of politics through which neoliberalism will be challenged.

Everything hinges on the discursive and affective register through which meaning is going to be assigned to the manifold democratic demands that characterize this 'populist moment'. The possibility of implementing counter-hegemonic practices to bring an end to the post-political consensus requires the construction of a political frontier. According to the left populist strategy, this frontier should be constructed in a 'populist' way, opposing the 'people' against the 'oligarchy', a confrontation in which the 'people' is constituted by the articulation of a variety of democratic demands. This 'people' is not to be understood as an empirical referent or a sociological category. It is a discursive construction resulting from a 'chain of equivalence' between heterogeneous demands whose unity is secured by the identification with a radical democratic conception of citizenship and a common opposition to the oligarchy, the forces that structurally impede the realization of the democratic project.

I have underlined the fact that the objective of a left populist strategy is not the establishment of a 'populist regime' but the construction of a collective subject apt to launch a political offensive in order to establish a new hegemonic formation within the liberal democratic framework. This new hegemonic formation should create the conditions for a recovery and deepening of democracy, but this process will follow different patterns according to the various national contexts.

What I am proposing is a specific strategy of construction of the political frontier and not a fully fledged political programme. Parties or movements adopting a left populist strategy can follow a diversity of trajectories; differences will exist among them and they do not have to be identified by that name. It is at the analytical level that they can be referred to as 'left populist'.

It is to be expected that this left populist strategy will be denounced by the sectors of the left who keep reducing politics to the contradiction of capital/labour and attribute an ontological privilege to the working class, presented as the vehicle for the socialist revolution. They will of course see it as a capitulation to 'bourgeois ideology'. There is no point in answering those criticisms that proceed from the very conception of politics against which I have been arguing.

But there are other types of objections worth taking into account. Given the very negative connotation conveyed by the term 'populism' in Western Europe, doubt has been raised from several quarters about the appropriateness of using it to qualify a type of politics which might possibly be more easily accepted under a different name. Why call it populist? What is to be gained by that? I would like to point out that this negative connotation is specific to the European context and, as I have earlier indicated, it corresponds to an attempt by the defenders of the post-political status quo to disqualify all the forces that challenge their claim that there is no alternative to neoliberal globalization. Such a pejorative label serves to present all those movements as a danger to democracy. In other contexts, however, 'populist movements' have been viewed in a positive way, as was for instance the case with the American People's Party born in 1891 which, as Michael Kazin explained in his book *The Populist Persuasion*,[1] defended progressive policies aimed at strengthening democracy. The People's Party did not last long, but the policies that it defended were adopted by the liberals and were influential in the New Deal.

Despite the emergence later in the US of an important current of right-wing populism, the term has remained open to positive uses, as we can see today with the wide appreciation of the politics of Bernie Sanders, whose strategy is clearly a left populist one.

Once it is granted that populism can provide a political strategy to strengthen democracy, we can begin to envisage the importance in the current Western European

1   Michael Kazin, *The Populist Persuasion: An American History* (New York: Basic Books, 1995).

conjuncture of re-signifying this term in a positive way, so as to make it available for designating the form of counter-hegemonic politics against the neoliberal order. In a post-democratic moment, when the recovery and radicalization of democracy is on the agenda, populism, by emphasizing the *demos* as an essential dimension of democracy, is particularly suited to qualify the political logic adapted to the conjuncture. Understood as a political strategy which underlines the need to draw a political frontier between the people and the oligarchy, it challenges the post-political view that identifies democracy with consensus. Furthermore, by referring to the construction of a collective will construed as an articulation of democratic demands, it acknowledges the need to take account of a variety of heterogeneous struggles, instead of envisaging the collective political subject exclusively in terms of 'class'.

Another decisive aspect of the populist strategy is its recognition of the role of the affective dimension in the political forms of identification and the importance of the mobilization of common affects, an aspect which is usually absent from the traditional forms of left politics. It is for all those reasons that, in the struggle to establish a new hegemonic formation, it is essential to adopt a 'populist' strategy.

But why call it 'left' populism? This is indeed the question that is raised by several people who agree on the need to foster a populist strategy aimed at the radicalization of democracy, but who question the convenience of qualifying it as 'left'. Some of them propose to speak rather of 'democratic' populism, others of 'progressive' populism or 'humanist' populism. Two reasons are usually given for the refusal to speak of 'left' populism. The first one is that, with the conversion to neoliberalism of the social-democratic parties – which are often identified with 'the left' – the left signifier has been totally discredited and has lost all progressive connotation. Since they do not want to be identified with the other type of left, the one claiming to represent the 'true' left, the advocates of the populist strategy prefer to discard the 'left' label. I share the concerns of those who want to underline the distinctiveness of the populist strategy with respect to the two current meanings of 'left', but I believe that speaking of left *populism* is sufficient to distinguish it from the usual understandings of the term.

There is another reason which is adduced to abandon this term: the fact that it is not suited to the transversal character of the populist strategy. It is claimed that in general the 'left' expresses the interests of specific socio-economic sectors and neglects demands that, according to the populist strategy, should be included in the construction of the collective will. I consider this to be a more substantial objection. In truth, when it is envisaged from a sociological perspective as representing the interests of determinate social groups, the notion of the left is not appropriate for qualifying a 'we', a 'people' resulting from the articulation of heterogeneous democratic demands. The construction of a 'people' in a transversal way, with the aim of creating a popular majority independent of previous political affiliations, is indeed what distinguishes the populist political frontier from the traditional one of left and right.

It is in that sense that the claim by movements like Podemos that they are 'neither left nor right' should be understood. Not in the sense that they are pursuing a politics without frontier, in the mode of the 'third way', but in the sense that they construct the frontier in a different manner. The problem is that such a position, by not making explicit the partisan way in which the 'people' is constructed, leaves unclear its political orientation.

It is to avoid this political indeterminacy that I believe that it is important to speak of 'left' populism in reference to another meaning of 'left', which concerns its axiological dimension and signals the values that it defends: equality and social justice. This is a dimension that I consider crucial to uphold in the formulation of a populist strategy aiming at radicalizing democracy. When it is recognized that the 'people' can be constructed in different ways, and that right-wing populist parties also construct a 'people', it is essential, for eminently *political* reasons, to indicate which kind of people one aims at constructing. Despite all the claims about their obsolescence, the metaphors of 'left' and 'right' still constitute in Western European societies key symbolic markers in political discourse and I do not think that it is judicious to abandon them. What is necessary is to restore the political nature of the confrontation and to re-signify the meaning of the left.

The left/right distinction can be visualized both as a cleavage and as a frontier. In our post-political times the difference between left and right is usually envisaged in terms of a 'cleavage' – that is, as a type of division which is not structured by an antagonism but signals a mere difference of position. Understood in that way, the left/right distinction is not suited to a project of radicalization of democracy. It is only when it is envisaged in terms of frontier, indicating the existence of an antagonism between the respective positions and the impossibility of a 'centre position', that this difference is formulated in a properly political way. I believe that this 'frontier effect' is more difficult to convey with notions like 'progressive' or 'democratic' populism and that 'left' populism brings more clearly to the fore the existence of an antagonism between the people and the oligarchy without which a hegemonic strategy cannot be formulated.

Instead of seeing the populist moment only as a threat to democracy, it is urgent to realize that it also offers the opportunity for its radicalization. To seize this opportunity it is vital to acknowledge that politics is by nature partisan and that it requires the construction of a frontier between 'we' and 'they'. It is only by restoring the agonistic character of democracy that it will be possible to mobilize affects and to create a collective will towards the deepening of the democratic ideals. Will this project succeed? There is of course no guarantee, but it would be a serious mistake to miss the chance provided by the current conjuncture.

Theoretical Appendix

An Anti-Essentialist Approach

There are two ways to envisage the domain of the political. The associative view sees it as the field of liberty and of acting in concert. Alternatively, the dissociative one conceives it as the field of conflict and antagonism.[1] My reflection partakes of the dissociative view and is informed by a theoretical approach developed in *Hegemony and Socialist Strategy*, according to which two key concepts are needed to address the question of the political: 'antagonism' and 'hegemony'.[2] Both notions point to the existence of a dimension of radical negativity that manifests itself in the ever-present possibility of antagonism. This impedes the full totalization of society

1 Such a distinction between associative and dissociative views is proposed by Oliver Marchart in *Post-Foundational Political Thought: Political Difference in Nancy, Lefort, Badiou and Laclau* (Edinburgh: Edinburgh University Press, 2007), pp. 38–44.

2 Ernesto Laclau and Chantal Mouffe, *Hegemony and Socialist Strategy: Towards a Radical Democratic Politics*, paperback edition (New York and London: Verso, 2014).

and forecloses the possibility of a society beyond division and power.

Society is seen as the product of a series of hegemonic practices whose aim is to establish order in a context of contingency. It is the realm of 'sedimented' practices – that is, practices that conceal the originary act of their contingent political institution and which are taken for granted as if they were self-grounded. Every social order is the temporary and precarious articulation of hegemonic practices whose aim is to establish order in a context of contingency. Hegemonic practices are the practices of articulation through which a given order is created and the meaning of social institutions is fixed.

Things could always have been otherwise and every order is predicated on the exclusion of other possibilities. It is always the expression of a particular configuration of power relations and it lacks an ultimate rational ground. What appears as the natural order is never the manifestation of a deeper objectivity that would be exterior to the practices that brought it into being. Every existing order is therefore susceptible to being challenged by counter-hegemonic practices, practices which attempt to disarticulate it in order to install another form of hegemony.

The second important tenet of the anti-essentialist approach is that the social agent is constituted by an ensemble of 'discursive positions' that can never be totally fixed in a closed system of differences. It is constructed by a diversity of discourses, among which there is no necessary relation but a constant movement of overdetermination and displacement. The 'identity' of such a multiple and contradictory subject is therefore always contingent, precarious, temporarily fixed at the intersection of those discourses and dependent on specific forms of identification.

It is therefore impossible to speak of the social agent as if we were dealing with a unified, homogeneous entity. We have rather to approach it as a plurality, dependent on the various subject positions through which it is constituted within various discursive formations, and to recognize that there is no *a priori*, necessary relation between the discourses that construct its different subject positions. This plurality, however, does not involve the coexistence of a plurality of subject positions, but the constant subversion and overdetermination of one by the others, which makes possible the generation of totalizing effects within a field characterized by open and determinate frontiers.

There is therefore a double movement: on the one hand, a movement of decentering which prevents the fixation of a set of positions around a pre-constituted point; on the other hand, and as a result of this essential non-fixity, the opposite movement: the institution of nodal points, partial fixations which limit the flux of the signified under the signifier. But this dialectic of non-fixity/fixation is possible only because fixity is not given beforehand, because no centre of subjectivity precedes the subject's identifications. For that reason we have to conceive the history of the subject as the history of his/her identifications and there is no concealed identity to be rescued beyond the latter.

To deny the existence of an *a priori*, necessary link between subject positions does not mean that there is no constant effort to establish between them historical, contingent and variable links. This type of link which establishes between various positions a contingent, unpredetermined relation is what is called an 'articulation'. Even though there is no necessary link between different subject positions, in the field of politics there are always discourses that try to provide an articulation from different standpoints.

For that reason every subject position is constituted within an essentially unstable discursive structure, since it is submitted to a variety of articulatory practices that constantly subvert and transform it. This is why there is no subject position whose link with others is definitively assured and, therefore, no social identity that would be fully and permanently acquired.

An Agonistic Conception of Democracy

After *Hegemony and Socialist Strategy*, an important part of my work has been dedicated to elaborating an alternative model of democratic politics able to give account of the ineradicability of antagonism and the hegemonic nature of politics.[3] The questions that I have addressed are the following: How to envisage democracy within the framework of our hegemonic approach? How can a democratic order acknowledge and manage the existence of conflicts that do not have a rational solution? How to conceive of democracy in a way that allows

---

3 I have developed this agonistic conception in the following books: *The Return of the Political* (New York and London: Verso, 1993, rev. ed. 2005); *The Democratic Paradox* (New York and London: Verso, 2000, rev. ed. 2009); *On the Political* (Abingdon, UK: Routledge, 2005); and *Agonistics: Thinking the World Politically* (New York and London: Verso, 2013).

in its midst a confrontation between conflicting hegemonic projects?

My answer to those questions is the agonistic model of democracy that I see as providing the analytic framework necessary to visualize the possibility of a democratic confrontation between hegemonic projects. In a nutshell, my argument goes as follows.

Once we acknowledge the dimension of 'the political', we begin to realize that one of the main challenges for pluralist liberal-democratic politics consists in trying to defuse the potential antagonism that exists in human relations so as to make human coexistence possible. Indeed, the fundamental question is not how to arrive at a consensus reached without exclusion, because this would require the construction of a 'we' that would not have a corresponding 'they'. This is impossible because the very condition for the constitution of a 'we' is the demarcation of a 'they'.

The crucial issue in a liberal-democratic regime, therefore, is how to establish this we/they distinction, which is constitutive of politics, in a way which is compatible with the recognition of pluralism. What is important is that conflict when it arises does not take the form of an 'antagonism' (struggle between enemies) but of an 'agonism' (struggle between adversaries). The agonistic confrontation is different from the antagonistic one, not because it allows for a possible consensus, but because the opponent is not considered an enemy to be destroyed but an adversary whose existence is perceived as legitimate. Her ideas will be fought with vigour but her right to defend them will never be questioned. The category of *enemy* does not disappear, however, for it remains pertinent with regard to those who, because they reject the conflictual consensus that constitutes the basis of a pluralist democracy, cannot form part of the agonistic struggle.

The question of the limits of pluralism is therefore a crucial one for democracy to address and there is no way to escape it. Asserting the constitutive character of social division and the impossibility of a final reconciliation, the agonistic perspective recognizes the necessary partisan character of democratic politics. By envisaging this confrontation in terms of adversaries and not on a friend/enemy mode, because that might lead to civil war, it allows such a confrontation to take place within democratic institutions.

This necessary confrontation is something that most liberal-democratic theorists have to elude, due to the inadequate way they envisage pluralism. While recognizing that we live in a world where a multiplicity of perspectives and values coexist and that it is impossible, for empirical reasons, that each of us would adopt them all, those theorists imagine that, brought together, these perspectives and values constitute a harmonious and non-conflictual ensemble. This type of thought is therefore incapable of accounting for the necessarily conflictual nature of pluralism, which stems from the impossibility of reconciling all points of view, and this is why it is bound to negate the political in its antagonistic dimension.

What is at stake in the agonistic struggle is the very configuration of power relations that structure a social order and the type of hegemony they construct. It is a confrontation between conflicting hegemonic projects that can never be reconciled rationally. The antagonistic dimension is therefore always present but it is enacted by means of a confrontation, whose procedures are accepted by the adversaries. Unlike the liberal models, such an agonistic perspective takes account of the fact that every social order is politically instituted and that the ground on which hegemonic interventions occur is never neutral, for it is always the product of previous hegemonic practices. It sees the public sphere as the battlefield on which hegemonic projects confront one another, with no possibility of a final reconciliation.

The distinction between *antagonism* (friend/enemy relation) and *agonism* (relation between adversaries) permits an understanding of why, contrary to what many democratic theorists believe, it is not necessary to negate the ineradicability of antagonism in order to visualize the establishment of a democratic order.

I contend that the agonistic confrontation, far from representing a danger to democracy, is in reality the very condition of its existence. Of course, democracy cannot survive without certain forms of consensus relating to allegiance to the ethico-political values that constitute its principles of legitimacy, and to the institutions in which these are inscribed. But it must also enable the agonistic expression of conflict, which requires that citizens genuinely have the possibility of choosing between real alternatives. A well-functioning democracy calls for a confrontation of democratic political positions. If this is missing, there is always the danger that this democratic confrontation will be replaced by a confrontation between nonnegotiable moral values or essentialist forms of identification.

Acknowledgements

In the elaboration of my conception of left populism, I am indebted to public discussions and private conversations with Íñigo Errejón, Jean-Luc Mélenchon, François Ruffin and Yannis Stavrakakis who, in different ways, have contributed to the development of my arguments.

For very helpful suggestions or comments on several aspects of the book I am grateful to Pauline Colonna D'istria, Leticia Sabsay, James Schneider and Christophe Ventura.

Finally, I would like to thank the Institute for Human Sciences in Vienna (IWM) for providing a very stimulating and congenial environment during the months, in spring 2017, when I wrote a substantial part of the manuscript.

Index

Althusser, Louis, 9
Austria
    Freedom Party (FPÖ), 18,
        19

Blair, Tony, 4, 32, 38
Bobbio, Norberto, 51
Boltanski, Luc, 33–4
Britain, 4, 25–38
    Labour Party, 4, 21, 25,
        26–7, 28–9, 35, 38
    London, 19, 25
    National Union of
        Mineworkers, 29
    New Labour, 32–3
    Tory Party, 25, 32
    Trilateral Commission
        (1975), 27
    UKIP (United Kingdom
        Independence Party), 23

Chiapello, Eve, 33–4

Corbyn, Jeremy, 21, 23, 38
Crouch, Colin, 13

Eastern Europe, 10
European Union, 20

France, 18, 23
    Front National, 18, 23
    La France Insoumise, 21,
        23, 67–8
    Nuit Debout, 19
French Revolution, 42
Freud, Sigmund, 72–3, 76

Germany
    Die Linke, 21
Giddens, Anthony, 4
Gramsci, Antonio, 2, 12,
        34, 41, 46–7, 61, 76,
        77
Greece, 20
    Aganakitsmenoi, 19

Synaspismos, 20
Syriza, 20

Habermas, Jürgen, 14
Haider, Jörg, 19
Hall, Stuart, 4, 30, 32, 35
Hardt, Michael, 53, 54, 55
Harvey, David, 50, 59
Hayek, Friedrich, 31
Huntington, Samuel, 27

Jaures, Jean, 46

Kazin, Michael, 81

Laclau, Ernesto, 1, 10–11,
    59, 63
Latin America, 10
Le Bon, Gustave, 62
Lefort, Claude, 42
Lehman Brothers, 12
Le Pen, Marine, 23
Lordon, Frédéric, 75

Machiavelli, Niccolò, 9, 65
Macpherson, CB, 14, 31
Macron, Emmanuel, 21
Mélenchon, Jean-Luc, 21,
    23
Momentum movement, 38

Negri, Antonio, 53, 54, 55
New Deal (US), 81
New Labour Party, 4

Occupy movement, 19

People's Party (US), 81
Portugal
    Bloco de Esquerda, 21

Rancière, Jacques, 13
Rorty, Richard, 75
Ruffin, François, 23

Sanders, Bernie, 81
Scargill, Arthur, 29
Schmitt, Carl, 14
Second World War, 11
Spain, 20
    Indignados, 19, 20, 41
    Partido Popular, 21
    Podemos, 20–21, 67–8,
        84

Spinoza, Baruch de, 73–4,
    75, 76, 78
Stavrakakis, Yannis, 74
Streeck, Wolfgang, 25–6

Thatcher, Margaret, 4,
    27–38, 44
Tocqueville, Alexis de, 42–3

United States, 12, 19
    People's Party, 83

Wittgenstein, Ludwig, 75, 76